Introduction

MARGINALITY, as those who attended this year's Southeast-
ern Theatre Conference's eighth annual *Theatre Symposium*
at Furman University learned, is an extremely slippery issue. Before the
end of the first day of the conference, participants—who had been invited to present papers on, discuss, and debate the topic of marginality
as it applies to the political, the popular, the personal, and the profane
in the theatre—had already begun to suspect that the original categories proposed were too narrow and exclusive. By the second day they
had begun to incorporate sportive, metatheatrical, religious, experimental, and community performance under the rubric "marginal," and by
the end of the symposium conferees were debating the merits, legitimacy, and cultural and aesthetic positions of such diverse and "extreme"
performance activities as Hacky Sack freestyle footbag, contemporary
haute couture, Philadelphia's Grand Federal Procession of 1788, and
barroom theatre.

The weekend's collective inquiry into marginality/centrality and the
complex, ever-fluctuating relationship between theatre(s) in the mainstream and those on the margins was initiated by Oscar Brockett in
the conference's first keynote paper. Subsequent keynote addresses by
Mark Weinberg and Kim Marra extended discussion into the areas of
community-based participation in the theatrical event and the radical
treatment of gender in the fin-de-siècle mainstream theatre respectively.
Brockett's and Weinberg's papers constitute part 1 of this volume.
Marra's paper was committed for publication prior to the conference
and will appear in *Staging Desire: Queer Readings of Leading Play-*

wrights, Critics, and Designers in American Theater History, to be published by the University of Michigan Press in 2000.

The remaining articles in this volume, selected by the *Theatre Symposium* editorial board serving as jury, are divided into two sections. "Marginality: Text/Theory/Author," which deals with textual and theoretical considerations, features articles by Jonathan Chambers, James M. Harding, Mark J. Charney, and Robert I. Lublin. The final section, "Marginality: Performance," examines performances or performance types that have at one time or another been marginalized and includes articles by Professors Mark E. Mallett, David Callaghan, Martha S. LoMonaco, John H. Houchin, Stanley Vincent Longman, and professional dramaturg and journalist Dan Friedman.

I wish to thank publicly the University of Virginia Department of Drama and Chair Bob Chapel for once again supporting the symposium with grant money. I want also to thank my associate editors, John Countryman and Andrea Nouryeh, for their invaluable help in preparing this volume.

JOHN W. FRICK
EDITOR

Margins and Centers

Oscar G. Brockett

T HE THEME OF THIS SYMPOSIUM—theatre at the margins—
like the themes of most symposia, provides a focus but at the
same time suggests an enormous range of inquiry. In fact one might
consider marginality applicable to most of theatre's history, for although
the focus here is on things at the edge, there has always been a mainstream or center around which margins cluster. Consequently, it is impossible to talk about margins without referring to centers. It is the
interrelationship of marginality and centrality that will be the subject
of this article.

The juxtaposition of margin and center raises provocative questions:
What intersections of power determine which theatrical works will be
accepted as central and which will be relegated to the margins, or ban-
ished to outer limbo? How many centers and margins exist and overlap
at any point in time? The subtitle of this symposium's theme lists four
categories of margins: the political, the popular, the personal, and the
profane. These categories offer many avenues for explorations and insights but do not exhaust the possibilities. In our age, perhaps in every
age, there are a large number of what Stanley Fish has called "interpretive communities" (1980, 322), each of which is defined in part by what
strategies it uses to interpret individual works, leading ultimately to decisions about centrality and marginality. Membership in one community
doesn't bar membership in additional communities, and membership is
never fixed.

Furthermore, decisions can be altered by time. Recently, while watching the 1936 film *Swing Time,* starring Fred Astaire and Ginger Rogers,
I was struck by how what was once a mainstream convention can easily

become marginalized. The film's plot progresses in a very predictable way, with songs and dances interspersed at regular intervals. Then, in a major and extended dance sequence, which has no plot significance except as a lavish, spectacular nightclub number, Astaire inexplicably appears in blackface. He is the only male in the sequence, which includes numerous female dancers dressed in black or white (although none wear blackface), and no dramatic point is made by Astaire's blackface. Would anyone today think of staging such a piece, except perhaps as satirical commentary on racial stereotypes? The dance sequence in *Swing Time* is clearly a remnant of a theatrical form—the minstrel show—that had certainly been popular (and I assume one could say mainstream) theatrical entertainment in the nineteenth century, traces of which survived into the 1930s in vaudeville and films through such popular performers as Al Jolson and Eddie Cantor. Where issues of centrality and marginality are concerned, then, we deal not with a fixed field but rather with one in constant motion. Consequently, it is wise to remain wary of any firm stand on margins and advisable to think of them as relative to a broad range of artistic and cultural forces.

To begin it is necessary to admit that on one level theatre itself is marginal- at least in comparison with the popularity and accessibility of other theatricalized modes. Although we should be pleased that many not-for-profit theatres are scattered throughout the country and that, despite predictions of decay and demise, theatre still survives (often quite impressively), we must also acknowledge that in comparison with the role it played a hundred years ago, theatre has been greatly diminished.

At the beginning of this century the theatre had very little competition; but after the introduction of silent films, radio, talking films, television, and various electronic modes, theatre has now been relegated to the status of a handcrafted product in an age of mass production. In other words, the industrial revolution that marginalized independent craftsmen in the nineteenth century caught up with theatre during the twentieth century as mechanized, mass-produced works (although they originally borrowed most of their dramatic devices from theatre) displaced or marginalized live theatre, at least for mass audiences. Although the statistics about theatregoing compiled each year by the Theatre Communications Group and the League of American Theaters and Producers are impressive, they quickly come into perspective if we ask how the percentage of those who watch television or attend movies compares to the percentage who attend theatrical performances. The answer strongly suggests that theatre is marginal in most people's lives. Although theatre professionals routinely judge the success of a live production by the number of performances it accumulates, years of nightly repetitions do not compile a record that can equal the audience reached by a single performance on television or by the countless reproduced copies of a film that can be shown throughout the world, with each showing being identical (at least in theory) to all the others of that particular work.

There are other ways of looking at this situation as well. One way seeks to distinguish among performances according to whether they are live or electronically recorded or transmitted. The difference is important. Live performances are repeatable but not reproducible. As theatre practitioners we tell ourselves (and I assume we believe) that in comparison to film and television, live performance has fundamentally different dynamics, which are based on the simultaneous presence of audience and performers in the same space—dynamics that cannot be duplicated by electronic or recorded performance. As Joseph Chaikin has said about the premises underlying the Open Theatre: "The only thing that makes the theatre different from movies and TV is this encounter with mortality . . . [t]he sense of being alive now in this room, in this place" (1969, 144). As much as theatre makers want to believe Chaikin's statement, however, experience indicates that the majority of Americans do not find such views sufficiently compelling to make them seek live theatrical performances instead of going to movies or watching television. If, however, we factor in as live performance various types of popular culture events, as many nowadays do, the balance changes quite markedly. Still, despite this, the differential is never overcome, in part because television often broadcasts live events.

All of this should remind us that we cannot address margins or centers without acknowledging the problem of definition. How we define *theatre* is crucial, for it specifies what is to be kept in and what is to be excluded. A definition works in two ways: first, it places something within a category; second, it seeks to differentiate it from all the other things in that category. It is both general and particular; it establishes both a center and boundaries. It is always easier to locate centers than to establish boundaries, for as we move away from the center, we find ourselves in increasingly unfamiliar territory. When do we run up against a boundary, and when do marginalized elements bleed over into some contiguous territory and make the limits of theatre indeterminate? Derrida and others in contemporary theory have warned us that in following any inquiry there will always be a residue of meaning left over, which, if we examine it, leads us through a process of deconstruction that can never arrive at closure of meaning.

I do not propose to deconstruct definitions of theatre, although I will discuss how some types of theatrical performance have been marginalized through definitions or implied definitions. Let me begin by pointing out that theatre historians have marginalized many varieties of theatre through implied (but not always stated) definitions. Foremost among these is the assumption that at its center theatre means the onstage performance of drama and that any other type of theatre is marginal. Many people have trouble conceiving of theatre except as the production of scripts and assume that the better the script, the better the theatre. Because of the perceived superiority of Greek and Elizabethan drama, more time has been spent studying Greek and Elizabethan theatre than any other. This promotes an essentially literary conception of theatre. I do not question the value of Greek and Elizabethan drama, and it is well to remember that one of the reasons why play scripts from the past have been so valued is that they are often the most concrete residue that we have of productions during those periods before there were reliable ways of documenting performances.

Despite this, however, we need to remember that theatre does not require scripts for its existence. Throughout history many (perhaps more) nonscripted than scripted performances have been presented to audiences as theatre. In English-language theatres from around 1700 to 1850, the evening's bill was liberally interspersed with variety acts—trained animals, acrobats, tightrope walkers, singers, dancers, and any other novelty (the more novel the better)—performed between the acts of plays. Critical thought certainly considered these insertions marginal, sometimes objectionable, but these varied activities were accepted as theatre. In the nineteenth century, as popular audiences grew, these entertainments were separated from drama and presented in their own theatres—music halls, vaudeville houses, and such—but they were still accepted as forms of theatre. Admittedly, they catered to debased popular taste, but nevertheless they often commanded audiences larger than those for Shakespeare and most certainly larger than those for Greek plays, which were very seldom staged. Distinctions between high (or elitist) culture and low (or popular) culture were acknowledged and accepted, and the popular was usually marginalized, at least by critics.

The distinctions between elitist and popular culture remained fairly clear until the 1960s, when the divisions began to be, and have increasingly been, questioned. Some of the most stimulating work in the theatre since around 1960 has emphasized elements other than a written text or script and has instead been more concerned with ever-expanding aspects of popular culture. The avant-garde and experimental theatres—such as the Open Theatre, the Performance Group, and the Living Theatre—which wished to foster change, did much to reinforce the idea that mainstream theatre is essentially a script-based, elitist institution that caters to a middle-class audience largely indifferent to issues of class, race, ethnicity, and gender.

Under the influence of popular culture, the concept of text itself has been radically redefined, no longer always implying a written or spoken script. Instead, text has come to be thought of as whatever is being presented or studied. It might range from a fashion show to figure skating or even to this occasion in which we are now participating (the 1999 Theatre Symposium at Furman University, 9–11 April). Currently in universities popular culture topics (usually subsumed under the heading of cultural studies) are often considered far more important than any concern for theatre, which is still often viewed as class-oriented and, because of its dependence on fictional scripts, inauthentic.

In a recent article in the *New York Times,* Edward Rothstein, one of the *Times*'s cultural critics, commented at length on how cultural studies in universities have become, as he puts it, "fodder for anthropological and political contemplation": "There is nothing today that is too Low for High thought: trailer parks, snuff films, Mickey Mouse. Some of this is because of the unparalleled power of American popular culture . . . and its aggressively democratic perspective. . . . In contemporary analyses, any distinctions between, say, a drama by Racine and a wrestling match with Hulk Hogan might be considered accidents of taste and class" (1999, 33). The same issue of the *Times*'s Arts and Leisure section included five articles on wrestling as entertainment and as an influence on performance and everyday behavior.

Critical and scholarly commentary on wrestling is not new. In the 1950s the French critic and theoretician Roland Barthes suggested in *Mythologies* that wrestling, through its iconography, is a reflection of significant concepts: "What is . . . displayed for the public is the great spectacle of Suffering, Defeat, and Justice. . . . What the public wants is the image of passion, not passion itself. There is no more a problem of truth in wrestling than in the theatre" (1972, 18–19). Jonathan Culler comments on Barthes's work: "Wrestling attracts Barthes for a number of reasons: it is a popular rather than a bourgeois pastime; it prefers scene to narrative, reveling in theatrical signifying gestures; and it is unabashedly artificial, not only in its signs of pain, anger and distress but even in its outcome: no one would be shocked to learn that matches are fixed" (1983, 38). Barthes's commentary is now some forty years old, but until recently most observers of popular culture viewed wrestling as something on the margins—as something aimed at a working-class audience with a taste for violence. When acknowledged, it was usually treated with condescension. Some commentators have even denounced its popularity as a sign of the disintegration of civilization and have linked it to insidious millennial forces. In recent years, however, wrestling's growing popularity has made it one of the most influential forms of entertainment and performance.

Social critics note that behavior in school yards, playgrounds, and parks reflects the kind of physical violence and win-at-all-cost strategies seen in (and frequently just outside) the ring. Professional wrestling's popularity may be explained, at least in part, by its visceral appeal; while watching, spectators find it difficult *not* to enter into it kinesthetically, and in turn these bodily responses trigger emotional responses, some of them elemental. To those valuing the degree of audience involvement achieved by wrestling, the theatre can seem especially staid and unexciting. Thus, in comparison to one of the most popular of popular culture forms, theatre (especially when thought of as restricted to the staging of scripted plays) has been pushed further toward the margins at the same time that wrestling and other popular culture forms have moved toward the center.

Perhaps one lesson might be that theatre should overcome its Victorian attitudes about appropriate audience behavior and encourage a return to the give-and take of earlier periods. The most commonly noted aspect of performances at the new Globe Theatre in London is the spirited interaction among spectators and performers, which was initially surprising but is now welcomed by the actors as stimulating spontaneity and alertness on their part and greater involvement from spectators. Peter Hall has remarked about performances in this theatre: "The essence of Shakespeare's drama is live interaction with a packed audience in a very small space in daylight, challenged to use their imaginations. There's nowhere else in Britain where that is happening" (Covington 1997, 68).

Wrestling is merely one instance in a trend toward using *performance* as a descriptive label for forms deviating from mainstream theatre (while borrowing heavily from it) and thereby contributing to the marginalization of theatre. As Michael Vanden Heuvel notes, performance "in recent years has been ordained as an autonomous art form, as an alternative to 'literary' drama" (1991, 5–6).

"Performance art" is now applied to such a wide variety of artistic endeavors that it has largely lost its usefulness, encompassing as it does works by visual artists, dancers, musicians, actors, and various mixed-art forms, all insisting on their status as live performance. Much of this work is at its core autobiographical, and this fact, combined with the physical presence of the creator/performer, seems to establish a claim of authenticity that some find lacking in traditional theatre. For many, the body itself has come to be thought of as the site of authenticity. Pieces by such actor/dramatists as Spalding Gray, Eric Bogosian, John Leguizamo, and even Anna Deveare Smith are valued in part because of this concept of authenticity, and it is interesting that their work is sometimes labeled performance art instead of theatre. A good example of the tendency to move certain kinds of performance out of the theatre category and into performance art is illustrated in the treatment of Marcel Marceau during his March 1999 performances in New York. Marceau's past appearances in New York were reviewed by the *New York Times*'s theatre critics; this time his work was reviewed twice (20 March 1999 and 22 March 1999) by the paper's dance critics and published under the heading: "Performance Art Review."

The point here is that theatre can be marginalized through restrictive conceptions of theatre, with the consequence that exciting work that moves beyond traditional theatre is often viewed not as an expansion of theatre but as new forms only incidentally or problematically related to theatre. In the 1970s, when Robert Wilson was creating his early works, among them *Deafman Glance* (1970) and *The Life and Times of Joseph Stalin* (1973), most critics did not know how to classify these pieces that scarcely existed in written form. The performance *was* the text, and if videos and detailed descriptions of these works had not been made at that time, they would have virtually disappeared. Wilson's juxtaposition of visual elements that created metaphorical and surrealist images were the most admired aspects of these pieces, leading critics to label them "scenic writing," "theatre of visions," or "theatre of images" (see Brecht 1978; Marranca 1977). Despite the passage of some thirty years, critics still have trouble categorizing Wilson's pieces.

Perhaps we should adopt John Cage's definition of theatre: "There are things to hear and things to see, and that's what theatre is" (Kostelanetz 1968, 51). One may conclude from this statement that Cage considers almost anything theatre, just as his ideas about criticism virtually eliminate marginality. In an interview with Cage, Richard Kostelanetz tried to get the composer to make some distinctions within his all-encompassing definition, asking, "Are some pieces better theatre than others?" Cage replied, "Why do you waste your time and mine by trying to get value judgments? Don't you see that when you get a value judgment, that's all you have. . . . The best criticism will be . . . the doing of your own work. . . . Your criticism . . . could be a piece of music or a scientific experiment or a trip to Japan or a trip to your local shopping market" (1968, 57–59). Cage was so convinced that the experience of art is individualized that he used the term "police work" to describe any insistence on the correctness of specific interpretations of or responses to an artwork or performance (Kostelanetz 1968, 56).

Cage's ideas point toward the self-consciousness about marginalizing elements that characterizes our time—the unfairness of being denied a place at the center or in the mainstream. We have become especially sensitive to perceptions of "identity" and "otherness" in various guises (race, class, gender, ethnicity, cultural norms). This sensitivity has led increasingly to interest in the intercultural, the cross-cultural, the interdisciplinary, and other interrelationships that imply differences but hold out the possibility of bridging previously accepted boundaries and bringing together subjects that have often been studied and practiced in isolation from each other. This development represents a conscious struggle to overcome marginalization by creating new "centers" through fusions of commonalities or relationships that have heretofore been unrecognized or ignored owing to suspicion of or indifference to the unknown or to barriers raised by academic disciplines and narrow specialties. To some in our field the current trend of opening out into (or invasions by, depending on one's point of view) other modes of study and practice seems liberating; to others it is threatening to hard-won academic or other territories. Whatever our present response, it seems clear that the study and practice of theatre are devoting a great deal more attention to the cultural forces that surround it.

Awareness of cultural forces and the struggle to overcome marginality almost always has at its core significant political issues—one of the subheadings of this symposium's theme. I assume that almost any use of theatre can be considered political, depending on how we analyze it. Even without searching for hidden personal agendas and unacknowledged power struggles, we can see that throughout theatre's existence it has been manipulated to support hierarchies of power and cultural ambitions. For example, ancient Athens, despite our tendency to idealize it, embodies this pattern. The very method of selecting what plays would be performed at the City Dionysia, the principal festival at which plays were presented, involved conscious or unconscious assertions of power. Available evidence indicates that the chief magistrate of Athens decided (on what basis and with whose input is unknown) which playwrights would be allowed to present plays (Pickard-Cambridge 1953, 79–88). This can be seen as a purely artistic decision, but it is not an entirely innocent one. In the fifth century, in addition to being a venue for plays, the City Dionysia was an occasion used by Athens to display its power and prestige. Delegates from other Greek states were invited, and the city displayed in the theatre the tribute (protection money, to put it bluntly) exacted from or willingly paid by other states under Athenian protection (Pickard-Cambridge 1953, 56–57). Aristophanes makes it clear that, because of the city's desire to put its best foot forward at this festival, he was chastised for including criticism of Athenian events or persons in his comedies and was urged to stage the more biting ones at another festival, the Lenaia, which was attended by few foreigners (see Aristophanes' *Acharnians,* ll. 504 ff., and *The Clouds,* ll. 520 ff.). I am not suggesting that there is anything sinister in Athens's seeking to present itself favorably. Its care may have led to the results that have made the city almost universally admired; but political forces were clearly involved.

There is still another marginalizing sidelight that we seldom consider. There were theatrical entertainments other than the plays done at festivals in Athens. We know from Plato and other sources that entertainers performed at banquets and elsewhere, and there is evidence that Greek comedy (including Aristophanes') descended at least in part from mime, a popular performance mode about which we know little because it was excluded from officially sanctioned and subsidized performances. That mime was marginalized is further indicated by the refusal of the Artists of Dionysus (the organization to which festival personnel belonged during later times in Greece) to admit mimes as members (Pickard-Cambridge 1953, 310). Thus, an apparently popular form of entertainment was consistently marginalized.

The virtual absence of mimes from the records of Greek drama illustrates in a rather extreme way the fate of most marginalized forms throughout history. Information is not preserved about performances considered unimportant. Because Greek tragedies and comedies were performed at state-sponsored festivals, official records were kept about these forms; but popular-culture forms that might tell us much about variant types of Greek theatre were excluded from official records, and consequently we remain largely ignorant about them.

From the beginning, then, political concerns played a major role in marginality, and throughout subsequent centuries European theatre had its center and margins defined politically, usually for the purpose of supporting governmental positions on what would be good for the general populace or what might incite behavior that would endanger the social order. In England in the 1720s and 1730s, for example, censorship had grown so lax that several playwrights, most notably John Gay and Henry Fielding, began writing highly satirical works about politics and public figures. Gay went so far in *The Beggar's Opera* (1728) as to have a character (the supposed author of the play) say that he had originally intended for the play to provide a strong and clear message:

that it was difficult to tell whether highway robbers were imitating government officials or whether government officials were imitating highway robbers. Not surprisingly, such plays were cited as justification for Parliament's enacting the Licensing Act of 1737. As a result, from that date until 1968 all plays in England were required to be licensed prior to performance.

Certainly this provision is well known to theatre academics, but what we tend to downplay is the significance of *who* was given the power to approve or disapprove of plays. This authority was given to the lord chamberlain, a nobleman whose principal responsibility was the management of the royal household and whose secondary duty was to serve as the arbiter of suitability for performance on the English stage. The implication was that plays should not include anything thought to be politically offensive to the country's ruler. The lord chamberlain was authorized to demand removal or alteration of specific wording; of passages relating to religion or morality; any mention of members of the royal family; anything that might provoke unrest in the populace; anything that might be offensive to governments with which England wished to maintain cordial relations; and a number of other things, many of which changed as time went by (for a detailed account see Stephens 1980). The government's concern was about what might be *said* in the plays and the goal always was to prevent anything considered offensive, for whatever reason, from reaching the stage.[1] Hence, the judgments were not artistic but political.

Because the lord chamberlain was also the licenser of theatres (a large number of which he authorized after 1800), he instituted a proviso that these new theatres not trespass on the rights of the three major companies. As a result, theatres came to be classified as major or minor, the latter being restricted to presenting clearly marginalized plays and marginalized dramatic forms.

Of course, one does not have to look to the past to find examples of politicized attempts to marginalize or forbid performances. One need look no further than the United States Congress and its dealings with the National Endowment for the Arts since the late 1980s. A law passed by Congress in 1990 demanded that, in evaluating applications for government grants, the NEA should consider "general standards of decency and respect for the diverse beliefs and values of the American public" (for provisions see Greenhouse 1998). In subsequent challenges to this

---

[1] Opponents of the National Endowment for the Arts would probably find these restrictions entirely just and desirable.

provision the Ninth Circuit Court declared the law unconstitutional, but in 1998 the Supreme Court of the United States reversed the lower court's decision and upheld the constitutionality of this law (for a summary of these events see Gussow 1998).

Reactions to the law and the Supreme Court's ruling varied according to attitudes about freedom of expression. One of the strongest reactions came from Mac Wellman, perhaps the most political of America's contemporary playwrights. He had earlier rejected mainstream theatre, most notably in a 1984 essay, the title of which, "The Theatre of Good Intentions," indicates his view of the ineffectiveness of mainstream theatre. He also describes himself as a marginalized playwright in relation to traditional theatre, for which he has little respect (Savran 1999, 17). His own work often satirizes American political stances, and he almost always thumbs his nose at would-be censors. Perhaps the most famous example of this is his dedication of his play *Sincerity Forever* (1990) to Senator Jesse Helms and the Reverend Donald Wildmon, director of the American Family Association. His dedication reads: "With my compliments, for the fine job you are doing of destroying civil liberties in These States." In 1998 Wellman, in an interview with Mel Gussow, reacted to the Supreme Court decision: "It's a political decision masking as one concerned with obscenity. What it is really about is marginalizing opinions that are different" (Gussow 1998).

David Rabe, although he has achieved acceptance in mainstream theatre, saw both the attacks on the NEA and the Supreme Court's decision as parts of "a recent manifestation of a fundamental hatred of art, of anything that does not coddle the public, that is not entertainment. . . . To suggest that things should rise or fall on the marketplace is a form of censorship" (ibid.). Rabe's remarks about the marketplace refer to those who have opposed government grants to the arts by insisting that good art should be able to support itself without subsidies. This group also defends itself by insisting that it does not wish to impose censorship but rather to question whether tax dollars should be spent supporting art that offends the taxpayer.

What many people found most unsettling was the failure of the law or the Supreme Court to specify *who* should establish the "general standards of decency" demanded by the law. By implication the standards would be those of a presumed majority made up of conventionally moral citizens who would reject anything considered obscene or avantgarde. Thus, unpopular ideas, perplexing artistic conventions, and anything that might make the general public uneasy—in other words, the kind of art often most in need of support—would be truly marginalized and be, as Rabe suggests, a victim of censorship.

Citizens of the United States pride themselves on not ever having had institutionalized government censorship as most other countries have. Nevertheless, some Americans have found ways of achieving de facto censorship. The most popular of these ways in recent years has been the intimidation of theatre companies. One path has been the threat of taking away subsidies. In Charlotte, North Carolina, a 1997 production by the Charlotte Repertory Theatre of *Angels in America* provoked the county council to cancel its subsidies for all the arts because it wanted to deny support to anything that justified homosexuality (see Nunns 1999). Similar actions have occurred in San Antonio, Texas; Anchorage, Alaska; and elsewhere. Among the strategies aimed at controlling what artworks will be presented for public consumption, the weapons of choice have been extended beyond cancellation of government subsidies to include boycotts (actual or threatened) of corporations that make grants to groups that present art thought to be offensive; picketing of theatres to oppose specific productions; and, in the case of Terrence McNally's *Corpus Christi* in 1998, threats of bombing the Manhattan Theatre Club should it proceed with its announced plans to present McNally's play (for a summary see Pogrebin 1998).

Such intimidation then is directed at the producers of theatre and their potential audiences, as well as at corporations that provide their financial support. The immediate effectiveness of such threats has varied widely. Its greatest, and most insidious, success has been achieved through increased self-censorship, as many companies have grown wary of producing works that might arouse controversy. Where this has happened, provocative pieces have been marginalized or ignored by those who formerly might have presented them. As a result, unwillingness to take chances on innovative or controversial works has become one of the major causes of marginalization in today's theatre.

This is especially unfortunate because adventurous theatre companies dedicated to exploring new and unfamiliar theatrical conventions and subjects are vital to the health of the theatre. During the 1960s and 1970s the margins of theatre were enlarged in a variety of ways by such groups as Mabou Mines, the Performance Group, the Wooster Group, and the Open Theatre, and much of what they accomplished was subsequently adapted and assimilated by the mainstream. Some of these groups still exist. The Wooster Group, for example, has consistently pursued its postmodern and deconstructionist explorations for some twenty-five years; but despite its critical reputation (both positive and negative), it remains marginal in comparison with mainstream theatre, although it still serves as a stimulant and inspiration for those who wish to pursue alternative modes. It does seem, nevertheless, that the avant-garde in the United States has become much more marginal than it was in preceding decades. Or perhaps because alternative theatres are now accepted as commonplace, they have achieved a different kind of marginality, based more on widespread indifference to their work than on a lack of adventurousness on their part.

Marginality as a *subject* has become a pervasive concern, certainly in critical writing and to a lesser degree in playwriting, where issues about identity, race, ethnicity, class, and gender are ubiquitous. Here I will confine myself to one example of plays dealing with marginality—*Slaughter City*, by Naomi Wallace. A complex play about the attempts of slaughterhouse workers to gain fair working conditions and fair wages from a management concerned only with profits, *Slaughter City* includes two characters who range through time over the past hundred years in brief scenes from American labor history that recall some of the most destructive attempts to silence workers. In addition, it situates most of its concerns around the body. Ron Daniels, who directed the first production of *Slaughter City*, says that in Wallace's work something is always being done to the body. "It is always being touched, caressed, burned, perforated, poured on and spat on. . . . For Naomi it has to do with making the body—for which read 'class'—burst its bounds . . . all in the name of change, hope, possibility" (Gornick 1997, 31).

In *Slaughter City* the workers are a mixture of male and female, black and white whose interrelationships reflect issues about class, race, and gender. The most interesting of these relationships is that of Roach, a black woman in her mid-thirties, and Brandon, a white man in his early twenties. Brandon is persistent and sincere in his attempt to establish a personal relationship with Roach, but she cannot bring herself to trust him because he is white, male, and some fifteen years younger than she is, all factors that she sees as sources of trouble. In the climactic, erotically charged scene of this ongoing jousting courtship, Roach discovers Brandon in the women's changing room smelling her dress. She demands that he put on her clothes and talk to her as if she were a man. After he acquiesces to her every request, she agrees that she will kiss him if he accepts her conditions. "If you can take this knife [the kind of heavy-duty knife they use in their slaughterhouse work] from me. (Beat.) But if either of us bleeds, if either one of us gets so much as a paper cut, it's over. And we'll never talk about it again. Agreed? (Beat.) Agreed?" After Brandon agrees, the stage directions read: "Roach puts the blade between her teeth. Slowly and carefully she passes the knife from her mouth to Brandon's mouth. In doing this, they are also in a 'kiss.' During this transfer, Brandon is pushed to his knees. He now holds the knife between his teeth as he kneels." Roach closes the scene with the remark: "That's where I like my Tarzan. On his knees" (Wallace 1996, 68–70).

Their relationship is short-lived, for Brandon is killed in an accident caused by the company's inadequate maintenance of equipment. The manager decides to try to avoid trouble with government inspectors by blaming Brandon's death on his failure to use appropriate safety equipment, even though the manager is told repeatedly by a subordinate that there is no safety equipment. Overall, the play suggests that on a personal level, despite an "edginess" that never disappears, gender and racial differences have a far better chance of reaching accommodation than class does because economic exploitation is more difficult to translate into the personal. In a theatre that values plays of substance, Naomi Wallace should be a figure of some importance, but to date she is little known among those who work in or study theatre. Her marginalization is a kind that must be overcome.

After this broad sweep of marginality and mainstream, I would like to end by suggesting that most of the forces that have marginalized theatre in some way also remind us of its power. Michael Vanden Heuvel has written that "despite assertions that we have moved . . . into the disempowering liberation of 'performance,' 'spectacle,' 'carnival,' 'play,' even 'life,' the fact remains that every attempt to transcend theater has served instead to restate" its power (1991, 233). Similarly, Herbert Blau, after considering several attempts to displace theatre, concludes: "As other disciplines try to open themselves to a prospective of infinite play, with the theater as a structural model, we can see only the possibilities of a newer theater from the perspectives inscribed upon us by the old" (1982, 74). As these statements suggest, theatre today is probably not as marginalized as it may at first seem. Perhaps we should recognize that the manifestations of theatre that are either embraced or marginalized change from one era to another and that one of the great strengths of theatre is that it persists and metamorphoses along with the culture in which it exists. In today's world, theatre (or at least theatrical elements) is pervasive, undergirding the vast range of performative activity. Thus, the theatre of today can be viewed as marginal (if we define it in very restricted formal terms) or central (if we acknowledge the theatrical base of almost all types of performance). How we choose to see it is a matter of perspective.

Works Cited

Barthes, Roland. 1972. *Mythologies.* Trans. Annette Lavers. New York: Hill and Wang. Originally published as *Mythologies* (Paris: Éditions du Seuil, 1957).

Blau, Herbert. 1982. *Blooded Thought*. New York: PAJ Publications.

Brecht, Stefan. 1978. *The Theatre of Visions: Robert Wilson*. Frankfurt am Main: Suhrkamp.

Chaikin, Joseph. 1969. "Interview/Fragments." *Drama Review* 13 (spring): 141–47.

Covington, Richard. 1997. "The Rebirth of Shakespeare's Globe." *Smithsonian* 28 (8 November): 64–75.

Culler, Jonathan. 1983. *Roland Barthes*. New York: Oxford University Press.

Fish, Stanley. 1980. *Is There a Text in This Class? The Authority of Interpretive Communities*. Cambridge: Harvard University Press.

Gornick, Vivian. 1997. "An American Exile in America." *New York Times Magazine*, 2 March, 27–31.

Greenhouse, Linda. 1998. "Justices Uphold Decency Test in Awarding Arts Grants, Backing Subjective Judgments." *New York Times*, 26 June, sec. A, p. 17, col. 1.

Gussow, Mel. 1998. "Artists See No Decency in Court Decision on Grants." *New York Times*, 2 July, sec. E, p. 1, col. 1.

Kostelanetz, Richard. 1968. *The Theatre of Mixed Means*. New York: Dial Press.

Marranca, Bonnie. 1977. *The Theatre of Images*. New York: Drama Book Specialists.

Nunns, Stephen. 1999. "Is Charlotte Burning?" *American Theatre*, February, 22–27, 74–77.

Pickard-Cambridge, A. W. 1953. *The Dramatic Festivals of Athens*. Oxford: Clarendon.

Pogrebin, Robin. 1998. "Play That Stirred Outcry Prepares for Its Opening." *New York Times*, 3 September, sec. E, p. 1, col. 5.

Rothstein, Edward. 1999. "Trolling 'Low' Culture for High-Flying Ideas: A Sport of Intellectuals." *New York Times*, 28 March, sec. 2, p. 33.

Savran, David. 1999. "The World According to Wellman." *American Theatre*, February, 16–21.

Stephens, John Russell. 1980. *The Censorship of English Drama, 1824–1901*. New York: Cambridge University Press.

Vanden Heuvel, Michael. 1991. *Performing Drama/Dramatizing Performance*. Ann Arbor: University of Michigan Press.

Wallace, Naomi. 1996. *Slaughter City*. London: Faber and Faber.

Community-Based Theatre

A Participatory Model for
Social Transformation

Mark S. Weinberg

To constrain examination of theatrical ideology to overtly political or issue plays "is to confine ideology in the theater too narrowly to the plane of the text, for like dramatic action, theatrical action—performance—occupies an ideological field" (Worthen 1989, 169). All theatre, by virtue of its being a cultural construct and therefore ideologically inscribed, is political. The operative definition of *political theatre* I will use in this article, however, is narrower. By political theatre I mean theatre that, by virtue of its creation and/or performance, seeks "to influence, however minutely, the general historical evolution of wider social and political realities" (Kershaw 1992, 1). Put another way, it is theatre that operates under the "assumption that the optimal relationship between theater and society is one in which theater, as a cultural practice, has an active role to play in the discovery, construction, maintenance, and critique of forms of sociality appropriate to that society" (Reinelt 1998, 283).

In other words, I will focus on theatre that seeks social change rather than stasis, transformation rather than consolidation of power, although I think it is possible to claim that the latter is far more prevalent and successful than the former. I will further limit my observations to one type of political theatre and one specific methodology.

Most discussions of political theatre focus on performance *for* an audience—observed theatre. In the introduction to their anthology *Staging Resistance* Jeanne Colleran and Jenny Spencer list three types of political theatre

> as a cultural practice that self-consciously operates at the level of interrogation, critique, and intervention, [but is] unable to stand outside the very

institutions and attitudes it seeks to change. . . . [1] theater as an act of political intervention taken *on behalf of* a designated population and having a specific political agenda; to [2] theater that *offers itself* as a public forum through plays with overtly political content; to [3] theater whose politics are covertly, or unwittingly, *on display,* inviting an actively critical stance from its audience. (1998, 1; emphasis mine)

They are talking about theatre *for* an audience, observed theatre.

After I had done such theatre for many years on university campuses, as a member of a collective, in labor temples, and for various social and activist organizations, "I came to believe," as Jan Cohen-Cruz put it, "that change was brought on more by people making theatre than by watching it" (1998, 5).

Obviously, politically charged theatre offers much of great value *for* spectators. I do not deny that, but:

- It is already given significant coverage. One can read (or hear, as we all have) about Anna Deveare Smith or Tim Miller, *Angels in America* or Bread and Puppet, Fornes or Gomez-Peña; but rarely do we get a chance to describe or theorize the work of David Feiner's Albany Park Theatre Project with poor teens in one of the roughest neighborhoods in Chicago; the Environmental Justice Project on "cancer alley" along the Mississippi; Geese's work with prison inmates; Marc Weinblatt's Boal-based empowerment work at the Seattle Public Theatre; Michael Rohd's "Hope Is Vital" work with teens confronted by drugs and AIDS; Norma Bowles's work with "queer street youth" in California; CTO Omaha's bringing Theatre of the Oppressed to businesses, small colleges, and loggers' camps; theatre making of the kind I am doing with children of the working poor at Boys and Girls' Clubs; Swamp Gravy; the American Festival Projects' long residencies and multipart community projects; Cornerstone; William and Mary College; and many others.[1]
- For the most part observed political theatre functions as an agenda-setting tool at a relatively easily discernible level, at least in terms of audience perception, awareness, and (with luck) even debate.
- Political theatre *for* audiences constructs and constitutes meaning with a level of spectator participation within the bounds of the horizon of expectations with which we are already familiar.
- Politically charged theatre *for* audiences often functions inadvertently as a tool of hegemony and stasis because it seems to promote the delegation of work toward social change to the players.

---

[1] See Rohd (1998) and Geer (1996) for information on some of the theatres mentioned.

An example will illustrate my last point. W. B. Worthen, discussing Marie Irene Fornes, notes that the power in *Fefu and Her Friends* comes from the fact that performances unseat the spectator and de-center the male gaze as the authenticating interpretive force, thereby reminding the audience of its interpretive power. Although this may be true, the question remains: does reminding the audience of its interpretive power in the construction of meaning translate into the audience's understanding of its constitutive power in terms of the event itself, or of the "real world" to which the performance event makes reference? The performer retains, if not authority and agency, certainly heightened legitimacy. I want to examine theatre that unseats the spectator and then embodies the subject position in the spectator-as-actor and his or her relationship to the audience.

Don't get me wrong. *Fefu* thrills me. I love politically charged theatre, although sometimes I despair of it. However, that is not my subject here. I am going to focus on community-based theatre and, at times, on the techniques of Augusto Boal's *Theatre of the Oppressed* as they contribute to community-based theatre development. By community-based theatre (often called simply community theatre in the United Kingdom) I mean theatre that closely allies itself with a particular community develops performances about that community's concerns, and involves some level of participation from community members, ranging from serving as interview subjects for story gathering to performing onstage. The final reason for discussing this type of theatre is, simply, that at some point we must evaluate political theatre by its impact and efficacy and I believe that community-based theatre far surpasses observed theatre in both.

I do not, in this claim, enjoy the support of all practitioners of community-based theatre. Bruce McConachie, reporting on a project he did with students and members of Roadside Theatre in the community around William and Mary College, although positive, is less idealistic than I am. McConachie (1998) examines the nature of community and its relationship to community-based theatre and concludes that although community-based theatre does lead to citizenship in terms of identification and participation, it does not necessarily lead to progressive change, regardless of intent and (in the performers' minds) clarity of presentation.

Raising questions about my own claims, I would also note that as significant as identity formation and community definition in the face of cultural homogenization are for empowerment, the results can be isolationist, and there is often a very conservative edge to a community's desire for self-determination.

I would maintain, however, that the following logic holds:

If citizens are participants in the art making, then the process will help guide their thinking in and out of the theatre.

The process in which they are involved reveals social systems and the images of such systems as constructs.

The process thereby empowers.

Now for the leap. Those empowered must be trusted. This statement is not an easy one to make for a highly trained, theoretically based, well-educated, thoughtful, and progressive-minded person *like myself,* who clearly knows better than the nontheatre people with whom I work (and from whom I have learned so much). It, nevertheless, is the essential last step.

Theatre, as bell hooks put it, "can be an agent for change . . . in liberatory ways, only if we start with a mind-set and a progressive politics that is fundamentally anticolonialist, that negates cultural imperialism in all its manifestations. . . . The fierce willingness to repudiate domination in a holistic manner is the starting point for progressive cultural revolution" (1994, 6).[2] Community-based participatory theatre is in some ways a repudiation of claims of superiority in aesthetic judgment, artistic virtuosity, political astuteness, and so forth. It may be difficult for those of us who spent many years training to let go, but if we see collaboration of this kind as an expansion of the experiential base of the activist artist, we can gain a great deal.

And let go many of us have, as a brief history of political theatre in the United States—beginning in the 1960s, when the legacy of pre–World War II political theatre was nearly forgotten—will illustrate. In the 1960s and 1970s political theatre was bolstered by and, in turn, bolstered countercultural activity and the galvanizing causes of the antiwar, civil rights, and women's movements. The utopian vision of companies, many collectively organized, assumed homogeneous audience desires and cultural groups that were clearly defined in terms of ideological perspective.

In the 1970s many companies began to lean toward more formalistic experimentation, regarding and battling form as the aesthetic culprit in the world of social oppression. By the 1980s artist-activists were often

---

[2]Although hooks was writing about cultural criticism, not theatre directly, this quotation applies equally to the theatre.

separated from the public and, although aesthetic idealism remained a driving force, "the totalizing radicalisms of the 1960s seemed to have lost their purchase" (Auslander 1992, 22).

Simultaneously, many theatre makers moved from insular communitarian and street groups to community-anchored companies. During the 1990s the culture wars over public taste, beliefs, and perceptions were replaced by an even greater movement toward the position of "citizen artist" (see Burnham and Durland 1998). Political theatre at the end of the millennium has been creating its own context and intervening in new places, both in terms of communities and actual performance venues. It is building on the 1960s and 1970s legacy of the "expansion of theatre in terms of: (1) where it takes place; (2) what is considered the core of the theatrical event; and (3) how fully the actor and spectator are involved" (Cohen-Cruz 1994, 110).

Regardless of the decade, though, political theatre has usually been marginalized by activists as separate from the ebb and flow of life and as therefore ineffective. It has also been marginalized by theatre professionals and scholars as just an aspect of "real" life, apart from the art of the theatre. The separation of ideology and aesthetics, on which these dismissals are based, has remained operative since the eighteenth century. Community-based theatre, particularly that which is participatory, continues to be devalued today using the same criteria. And yet I would maintain, again, that it is through this kind of theatre work, central to the lives of those it touches, that the goal of political theatre—the transformation of society—is most likely to begin.

What am I claiming community-based participatory theatre can do that allows it to be efficacious; how can I support such claims; and what are the dangers in such ideas? First, I claim that community-based theatre, often performed in venues primarily devoted to other activities, provides a reclamation of space. Dominant groups have always represented their dominance in the most accessible spaces—in parades on public streets, on billboards, in theme parks, and so forth. Community-based theatre reasserts the power of communal over commercial spaces.

Fredric Jameson writes that "the new political art [will require] some as yet unimaginable mode of representing . . . in which we may again begin to grasp our positioning as individual and collective subjects and regain a capacity to act and struggle which is at present neutralized by our spatial as well as our social confusion" (1991, 54). Community-based theatre is necessarily local. It is therefore theatre that reasserts and constructs physical and social space, thereby providing grounds from which to struggle.

In successful community-based performances, then, "ideally, the semiotics of location, space, and architecture work together to invite and include resident audience members as they reinforce ownership and frame elements of the community's identity" (Kuftinec 1996, 100).

Second, I claim that community-based theatre supports and perhaps even helps to create a sense of community in which people may participate as agents of change. Bruce McConachie notes,

> As real communities—cohesive social groups engaged in sustaining their members' identities through face-to-face interactions—dwindle in significance in people's everyday lives, the imaginative construction of "community" assumes greater importance. . . . Surely part of the reason for the success of grassroots theatres is that they provide images for their audiences that help them to do the symbolic work of including and excluding that constitutes community. No performance itself can alter the routines of everyday life, but community-based theatre can provide "what if" images of potential community, sparking the kind of imaginative work that must precede substantial changes in customary habits. (1998, 37–38)

I do not make this claim without harboring many doubts. We must certainly "scrutinize community-based theatre and the ways in which the collaborative process helps to build, perform, and destabilize community" (Kuftinec 1996, 91). For example, Kuftinec's study of the work of Cornerstone Theatre reminds us that "production work demonstrates the difficulty of using the term 'community' to imply stability or permanence. Thus, when [speaking] of the work as celebrating community or unifying the community, it is essential to bear in mind the unstable and temporary nature of this community, [and not to operate] with a certain idealism and mythology about the purpose and affective impact of the work" (Kuftinek 1996, 98).

I would maintain, however, that in the creation of a community-based performance, the structuring of the work reminds those involved that their everyday culture is a construct, full of difference and contestation, changeable without demanding homogeneity. The celebration of such local agency denies victim status and disavows an unalterable monolithic oppressor.

Third, I maintain that community-based theatre uses representation to challenge representation and narrativity. It raises the simple questions of who gets to make art and why. In community-based theatre, community members construct the representation of the community's own stories. Participants, in the midst of a most intimate connection to events, gain a distance from which to question narrative as an "inevitable series" and culture as "the way it is." Creative collaboration with others whose views of events differ reveals much about the force of social circumstances. Because the participant "is engaged fundamentally in the active construction of meaning as the performance event [which includes its development] proceeds," the performance is in a sense "'about' the production of meaning" (Kershaw 1992, 16). Unlike observed theatre, community-based theatre is resistant, not transgressive; rather than presenting counterrepresentations, it investigates the processes and apparatuses that control representations.

This is not to say that community-based theatre work will lead to intentional clarity and representational accuracy. In *Acting Out* Peggy Phelan persuasively demonstrates the "uncertainty at the level of the signifier" and the "unavoidability of misunderstanding" (1993, 17). I maintain that community-based theatre, particularly that informed by techniques of Theatre of the Oppressed, celebrates the uncertainty of the signifier and in so doing asserts the centrality of the dialogic and the power of participation, which actively constructs not only meaning but the event itself. It empowers and reveals. This empowerment and revelation in turn invigorate the creative community, which is heterogeneous by demonstration and imbued with contestation but productive and self-determined (at least within certain boundaries of influence) in the act of reading across the borders of otherness.

"The performances of community actors also suggest the instability of identity as constructed through social roles" (Kuftinec 1996, 101). The lack of experience of the actors makes it clear that they are both character and community member/artist, and so "the performance presents the unpresentable instabilities of individual identity" (ibid.). It promotes agency through ownership of the work, demystification of artistic creation and "talent," awareness of the construction of culture, and reassertion of contextualized identity.

Finally, I claim that embodied participation in the process of theatre making—performance itself—is the most subversive element in participatory community-based theatre. Participatory theatre mobilizes all resources—experiential and embodied, as well as intellectual—in the construction of meaning rather than in merely finding an index to it. Community-based theatre is a cultural construct and a means of cultural production.

The performative "acts out" (i.e., is, lives and relives, embodies) learning, which I see as reintegrative. By that I mean first, the performative act itself attacks the dualism at the heart of hegemonic practices in mass-mediated culture. Second, it attacks a repressive educational process that compartmentalizes not only knowledges but ways of knowing. On one hand, the system of doers and watchers privileges certain epistemological pairings and insists on a hierarchy of value for each; it also dispossesses both integrative choices and the crossing of boundaries that such choices entail. On the other hand, performative exploration is a way of achieving a sense of self as a subject among many—confused and contested perhaps, but still subjects.

Put another way, all theatre is not only political but potentially subversive (or at least resistant) because it is integrative and embodied. Moreover, theatre that allows all participants (or at least those who become designated representatives of others temporarily spectating) to perform allows the performance of integration and construction—that is, of power and possibility.

Even if one maintains that there is still a separation of performer-from-the-community and nonperformer,

> performers and audience members enjoy the dynamic oscillation between corporeality and signification in the embodied images they have constructed together in the theatre. . . . [It] is possible to hypothesize that audiences use the symbolic exchange of theatrical experience to make judgments about the kinds of images to include or exclude from their ideal community. Community-based theatre, then, is less about representing the realities of actual or historic communities—although markers of these realities need to be present to "authenticate" the experience—and more about imagining and constructing the relationships of an ethical community for the future. (McConachie 1998, 40–41)

If this is so, how much more efficacious, how much more fraught with possibility is the tension when the subjects are the bodies—when the imagined possibility is (re)presented by, acted out by, the body/person for whom it is imagined? If (put simply) the "we" is onstage? Theatre that puts community onstage—using various techniques (including TO, Playback, Hope Is Vital, EcoTheatre)—has the potential for the greatest impact and is in my estimation the core of today's most exciting socially active theatre.[3] Before going on I would like to provide a

---

[3] TO, Theatre of the Oppressed, is discussed below. Playback Theatre uses workshop participants to act out events described by other participants to explore their significance. Hope Is Vital uses an interactive approach that combines improvisational techniques, based in part on the work of Viola Spolin, with TO techniques to explore HIV and other public health issues with teens at risk. EcoTheatre uses interactive theatre practices to focus participants on environmental concerns.

brief introduction to the method I mentioned earlier—Theatre of the Oppressed—and then do some work that may substantiate or raise questions about the claims I have already made.

Theatre of the Oppressed provides a particularly attractive method for approaching community participants and for developing (even if only initially) a collaboration with performers. Augusto Boal's theory is based in part on the simple definition of oppression as having lost one's voice. To him monologue is oppressive; dialogue is liberating and productive. Theatre of the Oppressed is transformative, dialogic, participatory. It is best known for the *Forum Theatre* technique, in which a play developed in response to a particular community problem is performed for an audience that is then invited to intervene in a second performance of the same play to change the course of the action. Spectators become "spect-actors," and the performance becomes a rehearsal for transformation outside the theatre (see Boal 1979).

In her book *Theatricality* Elizabeth Burns discusses the notion of the audience's "horizon of expectations." This set of performative conventions—rhetorical conventions (the interaction between the performers and the spectators) and actualizing conventions (interaction among the characters, which implies a connection to the "real world" of the audience)—creates the framework within which observed theatre needs to remain in order to be successful (Burns 1972, 31–32). Theatre of the Oppressed challenges, yet uses, this framework within which performance is understood by blending conventions.

We do not have time to do a *forum* today,[4] but I would like to use the technique of *Image Theatre,* which illustrates "Boal's belief in the body as one's most essential tool in transforming physical sensations into communicable language and altering everyday space into a theatrical arena, or aesthetic space," to raise some issues (Schutzman and Cohen-Cruz 1994, 3). Realize that we are leaping into the exercises without the preparation that is a usual part of Theatre of the Oppressed work and that, because of time and spatial constraints, I am going to frame the activities a bit more tightly than I usually would.

[At this point participants were told to shake hands with the person nearest them and instructed that they were not allowed to release that hand until they held a second person's with their left hand, and so on.

---

[4]A short workshop was part of the presentation. The following paragraphs provide brief descriptions of the activities in the workshop but were not part of the paper as delivered. My remarks at the end of the miniworkshop were specific to the events and thus are only summarized in the last sentence of the description.

Within seconds the room was filled with noise and laughter as people negotiated desks and lecture-hall impediments to move about. Discussion in response to my question, "what happened during the exercise," raised issues of ownership of space, inhibitions and release, dependency and responsibility, and group membership, among others. The value of the exercise and the rapidity with which issues relevant to community-based theatre arose were illustrated.

To begin the next exercise, volunteers from the audience were asked to create an image of the experience of attending the symposium with their own bodies. The rest of the audience was asked to use their own bodies to expand a "sculpture" around the image with which they most resonated. Once everyone who desired to had moved into place, participants told the other people in their group what they thought the sculpture was about and why they had chosen to join that one in the first place. Postexercise discussion raised issues of physicality, clarity, the construction and contestation of meaning and identity, intention and interpretation, community cohesiveness and diversity, enjoyment, and even the coercion of limitations created by the situation and my instructions. Finally I briefly explained procedures for animating the images and developing them through improvisation.[5]]

I don't wish to make my claims easy to swallow. "The process of theatre, how the authority of the word, the presence of the performer, and the complicity of the silent spectator articulate dramatic play," must be thoroughly explored in community-based theatre (Worthen 1989, 167). I urge critical confrontation with the methods and rigorous theorizing about the work. Otherwise community-based theatre-making methods will be relegated to the quaint, will reproduce the very hierarchies they are designed to challenge or transform, or will become static and self-congratulatory.

What I can do for the moment, however, is ask your assistance as educators in the long-term work of such a rigorous critical examination. I ask you to consider redefining the curriculum in your theatre programs to include community-based theatre studies. I sometimes get the feeling that we have, by default, won the battle to expand the canon. Nobody knows anything anymore, so we have to provide many things to examine and question. Too often we provide only that which is distant. Community-based theatre work and study, by "recontextualizing of the familiar through the performative," can guide our students to agency through critical inquiry (Kuftinec 1996, 98).

---

[5]Both exercises are adapted from Boal 1992.

I am still a political-theatre maker. My stage now is most often the classroom. My method, whenever possible, is embodied and dialogic. Much of my students' work entails imagining alternatives—fighting the hegemony of globalization. Liberatory education is related in goal and action to community-based theatre, engaged in the decolonization of the imagination, thereby giving back to the student/audience/partici-pants the sense of choice, a reminder of the constructed nature of their agreed-upon reality, and of their ability to choose and change, to manu-facture a culture that is their own.

Works Cited

Auslander, Philip. 1992. *Presence and Resistance: Postmodernism and Cultural Politics in Contemporary American Performance*. Ann Arbor: University of Michigan Press.

Boal, Augusto. 1979. *Theatre of the Oppressed*. New York: Urizen Books.

———. 1992. *Games for Actors and Non-Actors*. New York: Routledge.

Bowles, Norma, ed. 1997. *Friendly Fire: An Anthology of 3 Plays by Queer Street Youth*. San Francisco: A. S. K. Theatre Projects.

Burnham, Linda Frye, and Steve Durland, eds. 1998. *The Citizen Artist: 20 Years of Art in the Public Arena*. Gardiner, N.Y.: Critical Press.

Burns, Elizabeth. 1972. *Theatricality: A Study of Convention in the Theatre and in Social Life*. White Plains, N.Y.: Longman.

Cohen-Cruz, Jan. 1994. "Mainstream or Margin? U.S. Activist Performance and Theatre of the Oppressed." In *Playing Boal: Theatre, Therapy, Activism*, ed. Mady Schutzman and Jan Cohen-Cruz. New York: Routledge.

———. 1998. Introduction to *Radical Street Performance: An International Anthology*, ed. Jan Cohen-Cruz. New York: Routledge.

Colleran, Jeanne, and Jenny S. Spencer. 1998. Introduction to *Staging Resistance: Essays on Political Theatre*, ed. Jeanne Colleran and Jenny Spencer. Ann Arbor: University of Michigan Press.

Geer, Richard Owen. 1996. "Out of Control in Colquitt: Swamp Gravy Makes Stone Soup." *Drama Review* 40 (summer): 103–30.

hooks, bell. 1994. Introduction to *Outlaw Culture: Resisting Representations*, ed. bell hooks. New York: Routledge.

Jameson, Fredric. 1991. *Postmodernism, or, The Cultural Logic of Late Capitalism*. Durham, N.C.: Duke University Press.

Kershaw, Baz. 1992. *The Politics of Performance: Radical Theatre as Cultural Intervention*. New York: Routledge.

Kuftinec, Sonja. 1996. "A Cornerstone for Rethinking Community Theatre." *Theatre Topics* 6 (March): 91–101.

McConachie, Bruce. 1998. "Approaching the 'Structures of Feeling' in Grass-roots Theatre." *Theatre Topics* 8 (March): 33–53.

Phelan, Peggy. 1993. *Acting Out: Feminist Performance.* Ann Arbor: University of Michigan Press.

Reinelt, Janelle. 1998. "Notes for a Radical Democratic Theater: Productive Crises and the Challenge of Indeterminacy." In *Staging Resistance: Essays on Political Theatre,* ed. Jeanne Colleran and Jenny S. Spencer. Ann Arbor: University of Michigan Press.

Rohd, Michael. 1998. *Theatre for Community, Conflict, and Dialogue: The Hope Is Vital Training Manual.* Portsmouth, N.H.: Heinemann.

Schutzman, Mady, and Jan Cohen-Cruz. 1994. Introduction to *Playing Boal: Theatre, Therapy, Activism,* ed. Mady Schutzman and Jan Cohen-Cruz. New York: Routledge.

Worthen, W. B. 1989. "*Still Playing Games:* Ideology and Performance in the Theatre of Irene Fornes." In *Feminine Focus: The New Women Playwrights,* ed. Enoch Brater, pp. 167–85. Oxford: Oxford University Press.

Staging the Dispossessed

Naomi Iizuka's *Polaroid Stories*

Jonathan Chambers

IN THE FOREWORD to *Humana Festival '97: The Complete Plays,* Actors Theatre of Louisville producing director Jon Jory offers this appropriate if not exhaustive description of American playwright Naomi Iizuka's script *Polaroid Stories:* "[*Polaroid Stories* is a] street theatre poem of emptiness, sensation, desire, and fear" (Jory 1997, vii). Employing a variety of theatrical and literary techniques, including free verse, a nonlinear frame, and a multilayered theatrical style involving both dramatic and epic devices, Iizuka has written a "haunting evocation of Ovid's [two-thousand-year-old epic poem] *Metamorphoses,* reimagined for the 1990s" (Dixon, n.d.). In *Polaroid Stories* the gods and mortals of classical mythology are reincarnated as young "speed-racers" and "neon girls" who scan for "pharmaceutical treasure," "drink from the river of forgetfulness," and echo in their words and deeds the ancient stories (Iizuka 1997, 187, 193, 202). Set on an abandoned and filthy pier at the edge of a city and played against "the sounds of [sirens, subways,] transistor radios, video arcades and a thousand collect phone calls in the night, [*Polaroid Stories*] transforms the chaotic life of a group of street kids, [drunks, pimps, drug addicts, and prostitutes] into a fierce elegy that casts new light on the depredating effect of street life in contemporary America" (Dixon, n.d.). Indeed, by fusing classical mythology with barbarous urban imagery Iizuka accomplishes no small feat. By way of seamless intertextuality, language that careens between gangsta rap and messianic lyricism, and character hybrids that are both compelling and distressing, Iizuka's street dwellers are transformed and given an epic grandeur.

In an effort to unpack the complex text that is *Polaroid Stories* I will endeavor to read the piece in the context of the "carnival" as theorized by Mikhail Bakhtin in his works *Problems of Dostoevsky's Poetics* and *Rabelais and His World*. Specifically, I will borrow and apply three of the key theoretical categories of the carnival sense of the world: *ambivalence, mésalliance,* and the *grotesque image of the body*. Although Bakhtin's theoretical categories were indeed originally conceived as a method specific to transposing the phenomenon of the carnival—as "syncretic pageantry of a ritualistic sort" (1984, 122)—into a method suitable for reading all forms of symbolic reversal created in the spirit of laughter in both literature and artistic imagery, his theory proves an invaluable methodology when one approaches a rich and complex work, such as *Polaroid Stories,* that includes juxtaposition, compilation, and hybridization of text, language, and character.

Some theoretical purists might question the prospect of employing Bakhtin's theory in a study not specific to a consideration of laughter or the concept of the carnival. In response I need only refer to the excellent study by Peter Stallybrass and Allon White, *The Politics and Poetics of Transgression,* wherein the authors endeavor to transpose "the Bakhtinian conception of the carnivalesque into a framework which makes it analytically powerful" (1986, 26) in studies outside the parameters of his original intent. It is in the tradition of this study that I posit this examination.

In the interest of academic honesty, however, as a final prefatory remark I should note two conditions that in some ways complicate the use of the concept of the carnival as an analytical tool. First, Bakhtin's theoretical categories—ambivalence, mésalliance, and the grotesque image of the body—do not exist in isolation. Instead, they entwine, overlap, and inform on one another within any given work. Second, these theoretical categories are to a certain degree similar in that they share notions of transgression, reordering, and inversion. These conditions notwithstanding, I wish to note two framing choices I have made that affect the structure of this study: (1) I have taken the liberty of abstracting the theoretical categories one from another, and (2) I have pigeon-holed or situated some elements in Iizuka's work under a particular Bakhtinian theoretical category that might well be discussed under another part of his rubric.

The impulse for Bakhtin's theory of carnivalistic ambivalence can be traced to the god Janus of Roman mythology. Janus, the deity of good beginnings and endings, is represented artistically with two faces. He is regularly associated with symbols (e.g., doors and gates) that suggest the variable or ambivalent quality of constant flux in rituals associated with transitions, both seasonal and personal. In *Problems of Dostoevsky's Poetics* Bakhtin cites the Janus-inspired mock crowning and decrowning of the festival king in the medieval carnival as the historical impulse behind literary or imagistic carnivalistic ambivalence that implies paired opposites, consciously chosen for contrast or for similarity:

> Under this ritual act of decrowning a king lies the very core of the carnival sense of the world—the pathos of shifts and changes, of death and renewal. Carnival is the festival of all-annihilating and all-renewing time. Thus might one express the basic concept of the carnival. . . . Crowning/decrowning is a dualistic ambivalent ritual, expressing the inevitability and at the same time the creative power of the shift and renewal, the joyful relativity of all structure and order, of all authority and all (hierarchical) position. Crowning already contains the idea of immanent decrowning: it is ambivalent from the very start. (1984, 124)

In his essay "Carnival and the Poetics of Reversal," Anthony Gash offers the following synopsis of the impulse that undergirds carnivalesque ambivalence. "Carnivalesque iconography implies a world derived not from a single divine authority but from a continuous interaction of opposing forces. Likewise, carnivalesque language subverts rhetorical claims to authority or objectivity by treating all language as dialogue" (1993, 91). Although many language or character determinants in *Polaroid Stories* could be analyzed via this notion of the "continuous interaction of opposing forces," this impulse is most apparent in the intertextual nature of the play script. Indeed, in bringing together the raw, hard-luck, street narratives of runaways and other members of the socially dispossessed with Ovid's canonized stories, Iizuka has uncovered by way of ambivalence some striking parallels within these two primary texts. The resulting intertextual text, *Polaroid Stories,* is a seamless work that rejects stylistic unity and is therefore not bound by the historical, cultural, or genre-specific limits of the primary texts. It can, as a result, foreground, heighten, and pose anew the ageless questions of mortality, existence, and fate present in both primary texts.

As a way of entry into the notion of ambivalence as seen through the intertextuality of *Polaroid Stories,* it is necessary to consider the objectives, both social and aesthetic, that Iizuka seeks as a playwright. In a recent profile in *American Theatre* Iizuka describes herself as a writer seeking to create "an event that happens in real time, a theatre event that sort of washes over and hits the audience as it struggles for a certain kind of honesty" (quoted in Berson 1988, 57). She continues:

I like theatre that startles me, and that makes me reappraise my relationship to the real. I think that's probably more readily accessed by going towards myth, or going towards something that's not, strictly speaking, realistic. . . . I do feel very much at home in the experimental theatre, where doing theatre isn't at all about careerism or money. . . . It's about taking risks. [She concludes that] theatre's interesting in part because it's not the main course in American entertainment. That can be very frustrating, but also very liberating. . . . You just have to make . . . theatre that speaks. (Berson 1988, 56–57)

Iizuka's intentions to explore the real in ways not purely realistic, specifically through myth, and to "make theatre that speaks" do not, of course, necessarily mark her as the only playwright to use intertextuality as a method. Indeed, many contemporary playwrights endeavor to deal with the real in ways not realistic and yet never explore intertextual techniques. Still, Iizuka's remarks are informative to this study because they reveal her willingness to go beyond the dominant realistic style as a way of exploring the real and to do so in a variety of ways. Given these factors, Iizuka is positioned in such a way that intertextual work is possible.

Although the *American Theatre* profile does not mention the word *intertextual*, it does note personality traits and artistic preferences that seem to predispose Iizuka to this dialogic method—eclectic influences such as contemporary playwrights Maria Irene Fornes (a constant force in the avant-garde); Adele Edling Shank (the consummate hyperrealist); and the Roman epic poet Catullus. Furthermore, Iizuka is an "avid" student of classical literature and the postmodern; she has drawn on extant texts before (her *Carthage* recasts Virgil's Dido and Aeneas as a couple in contemporary Los Angeles, and *Skin* rewrites Büchner's *Woyzeck*); and she describes her style as "synchronistic."

In the context of these observations Iizuka speaks of her process when she was writing *Polaroid Stories,* wherein the intertextual nature of the piece becomes clear:

I lived near an area where a lot of street kids congregated, kids who hopped freight trains and traveled a lot. I fell in with some of them and got to know them, and about the same time . . . [I] was commissioned to write a piece. [These kids] were very generous and told me a lot of things—it was like opening up this floodgate. Later they would actually sit with me while I was writing and look at my stuff and even correct me. . . . [The use of *Metamorphoses* as a framing device for these street kids' stories was] an intuitive connection. There is something about it that really fits, because the world of Ovid's piece is so mythic, and so terrifying and also at times really beautiful. There's something about the way these kids talked about stuff that's happened to them that seemed larger than life. (Berson 1988, 56–57)

This "window" into Iizuka's creative process reveals a dialogic impulse or "continuous interaction of opposing forces" (i.e., the two-thousand-year-old canonized text by Ovid and the raw, immediate, and unsanctified street stories) at the very heart of the text of *Polaroid Stories*. Thus, the Bakhtinian concept of ambivalence, which undergirds this impulse, enables Iizuka to achieve the objectives, both social and aesthetic, she holds as a playwright. Further, her deliberate multistyle approach to play construction not only frees her from the constraints of various genres, but it permits her subsequent mixing of high and low, serious and comic, sacred and profane within language and character drawing.

The second key Bakhtinian theoretical category to be considered in relation to Iizuka's piece is mésalliance. For Bakhtin mésalliance is the process whereby "[a]ll things that were once self-enclosed, disunified, distanced from one another by a noncarnivalistic hierarchical worldview are drawn into carnivalistic contrasts and combinations. Carnival brings together, unifies, weds, and combines the sacred with the profane, the lofty with the low, the great with the insignificant, the wise with the stupid" (1984, 123). Gash offers the following summary of mésalliance: "At festivals, people are liberated from criteria of estate, rank, age, and property status to enter into free and familiar contact in a shared space. Likewise parodies and profanities, oral, theatrical and written, combine and juxtapose the sacred with the profane, high and low styles, Latin and the vernacular, erudition and obscenity" (1993, 91). Iizuka's combining of vernacular and elevated language and of prose and verse are just two examples of mésalliance in *Polaroid Stories*.

As an example of the combining of raw vernacular and elevated language I offer this brief monologue delivered by the character D, or Dionysius, at the end of act 1:

> stories she told me, whispered to me like secret things,
> before i was born, before i ever remember—
> story of a girl who turned into an echo
> story of a girl who fell in love with a god
> and how she died and crossed the river of forgetting,
> how she heard this girl on the crossing, stranger on the other side,
> how this girl sang this song—
> sad song
> love song
> some kind of fucked up love song. (Iizuka 1997, 206–7)

Embedded in this short monologue are two impulses: shards of gleaming, sentimentalized poetry reminiscent of Ovid ("whispered to me like secret things"); and moments of harsh, unsentimental language drawn from contemporary street culture ("some kind of fucked up love song"). Although certain phrases, such as those mentioned above, appear to conform to and unquestionably belong to one impulse or the other, the whole of the monologue involves much language impossible to categorize. This inability to distinguish and separate where one impulse ends and another begins is typical mésalliance. To be sure, mésalliance favors a collaging over a compiling quality, wherein two contrasting impulses are brought together and liberated from the constraints of form. In short, as the binary construct unravels, taking with it all rules of form associated with those genres, a new seamless and independent form emerges.

This sense of seamlessness is also evident in the mésalliance of prose and poetry. Another D monologue, this one drawn from the beginning of the play, will serve to illustrate:

oklahoma boy likes speed,
he likes it cause it makes him go so fast
it makes him go fucking speedracer fast with them fucking speedracer
eyes.
one night, he rips me off, digs around in my stash,
i hear his fingers, i hear his eyes clicking in his head, i hear him
laughing in the dark
so high he can't hardly stand, he can't hardly breathe,
and then he takes my stuff, he goes away—
pockets full of quarters, he finds some arcade, video world is all
there is all there ever was, oklahoma boy disappears for days,
all speedracer eyes, big eyes, black as night, full of laser beams and
showers of light, galaxies and planets, whole worlds exploding in
his head, and it's so bright,
what it is, right, it's so bright, for a second you think you can see
then all there is is black. (Iizuka 1997, 189)

As with the combination of raw vernacular and elevated language, the mésalliance of prose and poetry involves dissolution of the rules that dictate those disparate literary genres. The result is a multilayered and dialogic form that involves impulses from both prose and verse. It is, in short, a literary style impossible to categorize within either of those preexisting literary genres.

The final key theoretical category from Bakhtin's method that I will consider is the grotesque image of the body. With the grotesque image of the body the carnivalesque practices of mésalliance and ambivalence are united and specifically aimed at the human body in an effort to annihilate the notion of harmony and proportion in the presentation of that form. According to Bakhtin, three strategies or instruments are at play within the grotesque image of the body: demonization—the abuse or degradation of a person, characteristic, or object; inversion— the continuous shifting of traits or characteristics from top to bottom and front to rear; and hybridization—the fusing of disparate people, characteristics, or objects into a new entity. Of these three instruments, hybridization is the most complex, producing "new combinations and strange instabilities in a given semiotic system" (Stallybrass and White 1986, 58). In short, with hybridization the audience's sense and sensibility are challenged by combining unlike people and/or characteristics into a singular form. In doing so the terms of being ascribed to the original figures within the binary construct are altered and supplanted by new terms as demanded by the new entity. Although all three instruments of the grotesque body are present in *Polaroid Stories*, hybridization is the most readily apparent. A brief recounting of Iizuka's character drawings will serve to illustrate this point.

There is Persephone, the queen of the dead, who for Iizuka is also a foul-mouthed crack mother and local junkie, D, or Dionysius, the god of wine and son of Zeus, a ruthless hustler who controls the flow of narcotics and sex on the pier; Orpheus and Eurydice, the mortal musician and the nymph, whose storied love in classical mythology withstood the power of death but who for Iizuka love, fight, drink, and drug in the shadow of a chain-link fence and eventually lose one another when Orpheus becomes so physically and verbally abusive that Eurydice chooses the "river of forgetfulness" (heroin) over love; Narcissus, the beautiful boy, now "raver" and adolescent prostitute, who rejects the love of the nymph Echo (now a "runaway girl, plain and unwashed") and is then condemned to fall in love with his own reflection; and Theseus and Ariadne, the hero of Athens and the princess of Crete, or, for Iizuka, Skinheadboy and Skinheadgirl, who are always "scheming and scamming, nickel diming what [they] can" and who eventually succumb to their drug addictions. The connections and misconnections on the pier are overseen by Philomel, "the girl without a tongue," who plays her "fucked-up love songs" and "stains the world red" with her blood; and G, or Zeus and Hades, a bifurcated god/character who represents both mortality and immortality and who sits in an omniscient position watching the transactions and dealings and occasionally joins his subjects in the urban squalor.

Grotesque hybridization, as postulated by Bakhtin, is defined succinctly by Stallybrass and White as the "inmixing of binary opposites, particularly of high and low, [so that] there is a heterodox merging of elements usually perceived as incompatible" (1986, 44). With *Polaroid Stories* Iizuka has taken two seemingly incompatible groups, one typically (for good or bad) deemed "high" and one "low," and blended them into a fascinating and complex hybrid. The ancient mythological figures, traditionally deified, are layered with traits that are typically read as unbecoming; and the contemporary street people, typically held at arm's length because of fear and/or repulsion, are imbued with traits that demand respect and empathy. In the process of hybridization the binary constructs that separate these two peoples collapse, and the independent, hybrid characters emerge. The resulting "new combination" challenges many preexisting senses and sensibilities.

Actors Theatre of Louisville literary manager Michael Dixon comments: "I thought in *Polaroid Stories* Naomi had a zapline to the Greeks through a kind of passion and obsession and desire that also applies to today's fringe culture of outcasts, runaways and drug addicts. Their sense of need and fear seemed a perfect match for the emotions of the Greek myths, but the contemporary setting and characters gave you a new understanding of those myths that was emotional and visceral, not academic" (Berson 1988, 56). In his review of the ATL production, critic William Mootz passionately echoed this thought:

> *Polaroid Stories* deals with the downtrodden, the dispossessed and the spiritually wounded in a way that refuses us the comfort of keeping them at arm's length. Just when we were on the verge of recoiling . . . [Iizuka's play] revealed those derelicts in a light that demanded compassion. By fusing the myths of Greek tragedy with fierce urban imagery, Iizuka achieves a miracle. . . . [S]he allows us to see these characters not as contemporary aberrations but as symbols of the ills that have plagued humankind since the beginning of time" (Mootz 1997).

In *Problems of Dostoevsky's Poetics* Bakhtin writes: "The laws, prohibitions, and restrictions that determine the structure of the ordinary [life], that is not carnival, are suspended during carnival" (1984, 122). With *Polaroid Stories* Naomi Iizuka succeeds in suspending the ordinary by way of carnivalistic methods. In doing so she has written a stirring and extraordinary piece that does indeed deal with "emptiness, sensation, desire, and fear" (1997, vii).

Works Cited

Bakhtin, Mikhail. 1968. *Rabelais and His World*. Trans. Helene Iswolsky. Cambridge, Mass.: MIT Press.

——. 1984. *Problems of Dostoevsky's Poetics.* Ed. and trans. Caryl Emerson. Minneapolis: University of Minnesota Press.

Berson, Misha. 1988. "Naomi Iizuka: Raising the Stakes. A Young Playwright Mixes the Lofty with the Lowly." *American Theatre* (September): 56–57.

Dixon, Michael Bigelow. N.d. Entry on the Actors Theatre of Louisville production of *Polaroid Stories.* In *The 23rd Annual Humana Festival of New Plays: A Festival History of Production and Publication Information.* Annual booklet [1997]. From February 1999 Web site listing <http://www.actorstheatre.org>.

Gash, Anthony. 1993. "Carnival and the Poetics of Reversal." In *New Directions in Theatre,* ed. Julian Hilton. New York: St. Martin's.

Iizuka, Naomi. 1997. *Polaroid Stories.* In *Humana Festival '97: The Complete Plays,* ed. Michael Bigelow Dixon and Liz Engelman, pp. 185–245. Lyme, N.H.: Smith and Kraus.

Jory, Jon. 1997. Foreword to *Humana Festival '97: The Complete Plays,* ed. Michael Bigelow Dixon and Liz Engelman. Lyme, N.H.: Smith and Kraus.

Mootz, William. 1997. "Curtain Call: *Polaroid Stories* Gave ATL Fest Moving Moment." Review of *Polaroid Stories. Louisville Courier-Journal,* 13 April, p. 1H.

Stallybrass, Peter, and Allon White. 1986, *The Politics and Poetics of Transgression.* London, Methuen.

Seduction, Stage, and Radical Sexual Identity

Artaud beyond the Margins of the Liberal Text

James M. Harding

WHERE THEATRE TURNS ITS ATTENTION to questions of sexual diversity, an aesthetic of defamiliarization tends to follow. The reason for this tendency is that an engagement with diversity necessitates an encounter with the Other, and such an encounter, if it is to have a critical impact, requires either a reassessment of those things that we assumed we knew or a response to those things that we confront for the first time. Inasmuch as the theatre facilitates such encounters, its aesthetic strategies tend either to make the strange familiar or the familiar strange. Although seeming to come from opposite ends of the spectrum, both of these strategies, when they are deployed effectively, yield similar results, namely a critical revision of the underlying assumptions and otherwise unchallenged categories that filter and give meaning to our experience and understanding of sexual identity. But as proven as these strategies generally may be (say in the work of Beckett or Brecht), their use by no means guarantees their effectiveness in cultivating an actual embrace or acceptance of diverse sexual identities. Indeed, in terms of sexual identity, making the strange familiar is unfortunately as potentially repressive as it might be liberating, for the borders separating acceptance from subtle appropriation and subordination are seldom precise or definitive.

Ideally, a theatrically facilitated encounter with diverse sexual desires would culminate in a recognition of those human experiences that the dominant heterosexual paradigms of our society otherwise elide, and in facilitating that recognition, the theatre would help to "recalibrate" those paradigms. Making the strange familiar would thus result in a re-structuring of the familiar. In this regard an encounter with the homo-erotic would transform the underlying presumptions governing the het-erosexual. Individual subject positions would shift, changing with the diversity they encounter.

Unfortunately, however, reality often differs from the ideal, perhaps more so than anyone wants to acknowledge. As a consequence, just as a performance may or may not live up to a text's potential, a staged encounter with diverse sexual desires may achieve little more than a recasting of the unfamiliar in familiar terms—that is, in terms with which one can safely (and heterosexually) identify. Rather than actually subverting heterosexual presumptions and rather than actually laying the foundation for an embrace of sexual diversity, the result far too often amounts to a pernicious form of lip service and a repressive perpetua-tion of heterosexual imperative that masquerades as acceptance of sex-ual diversity. It is especially pernicious, above all, because the masquer-ade is neither conscious nor deliberate.

That masquerade has everything to do with the conflict between text and performance. Indeed, the troublesome relation of text to perform-ance has a direct relevance on how we conceptualize what passes for an acceptance and/or an embrace of sexual diversity. To characterize such conceptualizations as a form of masquerade (as I do here) is to draw attention to "slippages" that allow for a textually articulated embrace of sexual diversity on the one hand and an avoidance of that diversity at the level of performance on the other. This is not intended to suggest a blatant hypocrisy but rather to suggest that the always-looming po-tential disparity between a progressive textual stance and a regressive enactment of that same stance ought to make us suspicious of the writ-ten word as a site for cultivating acceptance and embrace of diverse sexual identities. The characterization as a masquerade is thus intended to expose naive illusions of acceptance. It is intended to focus attention on the ways that the written word seduces us into believing that we have achieved what in deed, act, and performance we have not.

The issue here is not one of a mere failure to live up to the ideals and standards that we and our open-minded predecessors have codified in the written word, something tantamount to what one might describe as a poor performance of a well-composed dramatic text. The notion of performance developed in the following arguments, much like that affirmed recently by Bill Worthen, is positioned decisively at odds with "a desire to locate the meanings of the stage in the contours of the dramatic text" (Worthen 1998, 1093). It is, in other words, positioned at odds with a desire to locate the performance of acceptance of sexual diversity in the contours of written statements, pronouncements, manifestoes or any other *literary* expressions. I place little stock or hope in any of these textual forms, despite an enduring and sincere commitment to the teaching of literature. Just as Worthen poses the rhetorical question, "How can performance studies help move the literary conception of drama beyond the incapacitating notion of performance as a version of the text?" (Worthen 1998, 1095), this essay both poses and would answer the question, *How can a performance-based understanding of acceptance help to move our embrace of diverse sexual identities beyond the ambiguous, unstable affirmations of the written word?*

Expressing suspicions about the printed word is nothing particularly new. The suspicions are but echoes of similar sentiments that surfaced in the period of modernism, and although influenced on a more general level by what Raymond Williams has described as modernism's "radical questioning of the process of representation, [by its] break with the . . . view that language is either a clear, transparent glass or a mirror" (1989, 49), these expressed suspicions are more specifically related to the antitextual traditions that emerge and gain acceptance in modern experimental or avant-garde theatre. Those theatrical traditions arguably found their most influential voice in the work of Antonin Artaud. For this reason, in the following comments a discussion of Artaud's seminal theoretical work, *The Theater and Its Double* (first published in 1938), frames the paper's larger concern with the relation that the avant-garde's antitextual traditions have to issues of sexual diversity. Before moving into that discussion, however, a momentary digression would seem in order, if for no other reason than to acknowledge that the antitextual traditions of the avant-garde did not develop in a vacuum.

The antitextualism of the avant-garde unfolded within a larger climate of theatrical experimentation that not only challenged the subordinate relation of performance to text but also challenged the subordinate relation of audience to stage. Its antitextualism was matched by, indeed was coordinated with, repeated attempts to abolish the boundaries separating audience from performers. Yet such attempts were usually not ends in themselves but rather a kind of necessary prerequisite or a springboard of sorts for a calculated theatrical event. Although the historical avant-garde had a taste for the outrageous and a cultivated desire to "shock the bourgeois," by and large its performances were tailored to specific audiences—audiences that, for all their officially expressed shock and indignation, were nonetheless predisposed to serve as conduits for avant-garde performances and for the avant-garde's antitextualism. In short, the avant-garde could not have done what it did without the audience that it courted.[1]

Some sense of the dynamic that the avant-garde had with its intended audience is relevant to the present discussion because the following argument itself is tailored to a specific audience. There is, for example, little effort given to trying to change the views of those whose beliefs or moral sensibilities preclude a legitimate place for homosexual identities. This is by no means a dismissal of the need to mount a vigilant resistance to discrimination couched in moral imperatives, but the arguments here are more specifically directed toward those who already consider themselves allies of other members of society whose sexual identities differ from their own. In this particular instance the primary audience is composed of heterosexuals who are presumably open to diverse sexual identities. The audience also includes homosexuals as well, for the majority of what follows is an attempt to decisively "step out" of and beyond the presumptions of the dominant heterosexual culture in their direction.

These presumptions, then, constantly reassert themselves, and hence the underlying assumption of this paper is that for heterosexual critics working within the discursive and institutional structures of a society that presumes, if not enforces, a heterosexual norm (i.e., a society based on what has often been called compulsory heterosexuality), even these critics' most progressive convictions will slowly gravitate back into the dominant heterosexual culture from which they speak. The acceptance and embrace of sexual diversity is thus a daunting challenge in need of constant reassessment, recuperation, and recovery. Much of that challenge involves developing strategies that circumvent the almost unavoidable regression of insight into cliché and of progressive open-mindedness into hollow slogan mongering.

Although the work of Artaud is not specifically concerned with matters pertaining to sexual diversity per se, it does lay the conceptual groundwork for a strategy that, at the very least, mounts some resistance to the "gravitational" pull of heterosexual culture. It is a strategy that ultimately locates the emergence of cliché and slogan mongering within the realms of repetition, representation, and the written word, and it is at the core of Artaud's seminal work on the theatre. In the most decisively antitextual segment of *The Theater and Its Double,* the chapter titled "No More Masterpieces," Artaud identifies what he considers the

---

[1] Audiences were also capable of shutting down the avant-garde, as the Fascists proved when they came to power in the thirties.

authentic theatre and locates it in the realm of immediate performance, a realm that he positions in direct opposition to re-presentation and the written word. Locating the authentic within the realms of the ephemeral, the singular, and the unique, Artaud argues:

> Let us . . . recognize that what has been said is not still to be said; that an expression does not have the same value twice, does not live two lives; that all words, once spoken, are dead and function only at the moment when they are uttered, that a form, once it has served, cannot be used again and asks only to be replaced by another, and that the theater is the only place in the world where a gesture, once made, can never be made the same way twice.
>
> If the public does not frequent our literary masterpieces, it is because those masterpieces are literary, that is to say fixed; and fixed in forms that no longer respond to the needs of the time. (1958 [1938], 75)

What emerges from Artaud's comments is a radical sense of space and time and an awareness of the ravaging effect that history has on those expressions that, because they were profound in their initial articulation, we treasure most highly. Although one might take issue with the notion that "words, once spoken, are dead," the subsequent functions that they assume certainly do not have "the same value twice." In fact, they often assume the opposite value. Recognition of this temporal inverting "slippage" is in many respects the cornerstone of the propositions to follow—propositions that allow us to claim the following: in the politics of sexual diversity, words, once spoken, easily lend themselves to appropriation. Indeed, it is one of the great tragedies of language itself that we who are its practitioners, its craftsmen and -women, have proven incapable of forging a progressive discourse—be it philosophical, political, religious, or literary—that with the smallest passage of time cannot be appropriated and deployed in the pursuit of opposite, repressive ends.

For Artaud this radical sense of history and its ravaging effects led him into an increasing reliance on the immediacy of performance—a reliance so uncompromising that Jacques Derrida cites it as one of the rare instances of Western culture that actually circumvents representation. Derrida argues that if contemporary theatrical audacity "declares its fidelity to Artaud, then the question of the theater of cruelty . . . has the value of a historic question . . . [that] is historic in an absolute and radical sense . . . [because] it announces the limit of representation" (1978, 233–34). In this respect Artaud's notion of performance is an anomaly in the history of the theatre because it envisions the theatre not as an arena for the enactment or performance of a (dramatic) text but as one that is fundamentally suspicious of text as a repressive authority. Artaud is quite explicit on this point, as his comments in his chapter "Letters on Language" attest: "Here is what seems to me an elementary truth that must precede any other: namely, that the theater, an independent and autonomous art, must, in order to revive or simply to live, realize what differentiates it from text, pure speech, literature and all other fixed and written means" (1958 [1938], 106).

The call to envision theatre as being set in opposition to "fixed and written means," a call that in many respects has become a signature gesture of the avant-garde, reconceives the theatre not as an arena for the representation of life but as a locus for "break[ing] through language in order to touch life" itself (Artaud 1958 [1938], 13). This vision of the theatre, where life and art are no longer separate, where artistic gesture is a living, immediate end in itself, conceptualizes all meaning as ephemeral and delimited by specific moments of performance—moments that codification into text necessarily vitiates and nullifies. Such a vision of language and meaning, of textuality and performance, has profound implications for how we conceptualize our notions of acceptance and embrace of sexual diversity.

Following Artaud's lead then, acceptance and embrace are understood here as performative acts in the Artaudean sense. They are, above all, acts fundamentally differentiated from text and "all other fixed and written means," and as performative acts, acceptance and embrace are, like theatrical events, ephemeral and fleeting. Their authenticity—indeed the very concept of authenticity itself—arguably needs to be understood as a temporal category subject to unavoidable erosion and demise. The embrace of sexual diversity, the acceptance of sexual difference, is not a result of some lasting moment of enlightenment but is rather an ever-expiring sequence of acceptances, each individual moment of which is delimited by the contextual particulars of its enactment and each individual moment of which is subject to appropriation and reintegration into the repressive, heterosexual normative tendencies that dominate our society. Artaud's arguments press upon us the need, in the name of acceptance and embrace, to cruelly and unsympathetically turn on all our previous moments of acceptance before those very moments draw us into the oppressive ranks of the intolerant, ranks all the more oppressive because they are armed with the hollow rhetoric of inclusiveness—hollow like a Trojan horse.

Where these assertions about the ephemeral nature of acceptance and embrace intersect with Artaud's vision of the theatre is in their preference for flux over fixity and for performance over text. But if it is easy to find in Artaud's work the most emphatic admonishments against the paralyzing, deadening effects of what he calls our "superstitious valuation of texts and *written* poetry" (1958 [1938], 78 [emphasis in original]), his concept of performance proves to be more elusive (which at one level perhaps it needs to be). However, because the acceptance and embrace of sexual diversity is positioned within the realms of immediacy and performance, it is imperative that we seek some sense of what this performance "beyond flux and ephemerality" actually is. An indication of this surfaces in Artaud's belief that "the encounter upon the stage of two passionate manifestations, two living centers, two nervous magnetisms is something as entire, true, even decisive, as, in life, the encounter of one epidermis with another in a timeless debauchery" (1958 [1938], 79). It is worth underscoring the extent to which Artaud, in his use of the term *debauchery,* associates his notion of performance with the erotic.

For Artaud the departure from fixed discursive and institutional forms is perhaps best exemplified in the fleeting moments of our own sexual gratification, moments that, much like our need for sustenance, compel us forward as these gratifications inevitably fade, subsiding and giving way to the surge of new desires and to the pursuit of new gratifications. Not only does Artaud "propose to return through the theater to an idea of physical knowledge of images," but he admonishes us as well (even in the opening pages of his book) "not to waste in the sole concern for eating our simple power of being hungry" (1958 [1938], 7, 80). It is not difficult to find in these visceral images Artaud's warning against the lull of complacency and self-satisfaction, but in doing so one needs to be cautious not to overlook how radically "the physical knowledge" to which Artaud alludes is positioned at odds with all of our inculcated notions of propriety. So radical is this "physical knowledge," in fact, that in portraying it Artaud confronts us with the image of someone in the time of the plague casting all rational caution to the wind, experiencing "the surge of erotic fever" and "trying to wrench a criminal pleasure from the dying or even the dead, half crushed under the pile of corpses where chance has lodged them" (1958 [1938], 24).

With regard to questions of sexual diversity and homoerotic desire, Artaud's admonishments push us in new directions. Inasmuch as he chides us "because we choose to observe our acts and lose ourselves in considerations of their imagined form instead of being impelled by their force" (1958 [1938], 8), he casts a gauntlet before those of us who base our acceptance of homosexuality on some abstract notion of what homosexuality must be. How then shall we measure our openness to sexual diversity, not in some imagined general sense but in an actual sense? We need to look not to the politics, but rather to the erotics, of acceptance.

We need to look to seduction and to our openness to desire—homo-erotic desire. If Artaud's admonishments are at all relevant to such ques-tions, then we have to look at his contrast (and allow the adaptation of his statements here) between what we imagine the form of homoerotic desire to be and what it means to be "impelled by . . . [the] force" of that desire—in short, by what it means to be seduced by that desire. Inasmuch as Artaud contrasts the stultifying fixity of abstract notions with the fleeting, visceral experience of hunger, yearning, and "the surge of erotic fever," he lays the foundation for what amounts to a radical alteration not only in our sexual politics but, more important, in our individual sexual identities. This is a decisively antiessentialist prescription, one that genuinely tests the tenor of our lip service to antiessentialism because it begins first at home in the security (or inse-curity) of our own sexual identities.

It is difficult to imagine anyone arguing that her or his embrace of heterosexuality is the result of compelling pieces of writing. On the contrary, it is grounded in a socially conditioned openness to seduc-tion—despite the fact that individual commitments to partners often lead to an avoidance of situations where seduction and desire would progress to gratification and potentially put existing relationships at risk. But desire surfaces nonetheless, not in any fixed, essential, or en-during form but rather in the fleeting, ephemeral mood that accentuates passage from one situation or context to the next. In this regard rein-forcement of heterosexual identity gratification is not the issue but is instead "the simple power of being hungry"—a power that can only emerge within contexts and environments that stimulate hunger. So too with the experience of homoerotic desire, with an openness to homo-erotic seduction. The question of acceptance and embrace is not an-swered in abstract formulations, in written texts, or necessarily even in a consummating sexual act but rather in the fleeting moments of desire and in "the simple power of being hungry." As is the case with those seductive heterosexual moments, the seductiveness of the homoerotic can only coalesce in environments and amid dispositions that are con-ducive to seduction, and those environments are ephemeral and need repeatedly to be reconstituted.

Works Cited

Artaud, Antonin. 1958. *The Theater and Its Double*. Trans. Mary Caroline Richards. New York: Grove Press. Originally published as *Le théâtre et son double* (Paris: Gallimard, 1938).

Derrida, Jacques. 1978. *Writing and Difference*. Chicago: University of Chicago Press.

Williams, Raymond. 1989. "What Was Modernism?" *New Left Review* 175: 48–52.

Worthen, W. B. 1998. "Drama, Performativity, and Performance." *PMLA* 113 (October): 1093–1107.

Transcending the Limits

of the Word

Montage and Margins in
Caryl Churchill's *Cloud Nine*

Mark J. Charney

IN SPITE OF THE FACT that British dramatist Caryl Churchill wrote her most acclaimed play, *Cloud Nine*, in 1979, it remains twenty years later an original and controversial text rooted firmly outside the mainstream—one that is primarily performed by theatres in cities and at universities that dare to produce avant-garde and postmodern drama. Churchill's overt examination of sexual politics as metaphor for social criticism, gender exploration, and even race relations asks its audience to become actively involved in deciphering meaning from a play that denies conventional narrative and traditional character development. Not only does the work resist genre categorization—it cannot easily be labeled realistic, absurd, or even historically avant-garde—but its emphasis on the postmodern use of gender bending in casting, of layering, and of anachronism also purposely confuses audiences, especially given the stylistic, temporal, and spatial distinctions between acts 1 and 2. Because of the challenging nature of the varied themes Churchill addresses and the experimental and original format in which she chooses to express these themes, *Cloud Nine* is a play that will always remain relegated to the margins, even as the margins shift, change, and broaden.

One of the most successful ways to read or interpret such a text, then, involves abstracting its experiments with structure and form, where Churchill initiates many of the play's most striking challenges to linearity and traditional chronology. Her primary guiding structural metaphor is the dialectic, setting up parallel and often nonparallel opposing forces in the same act. In *Cloud Nine* Churchill treats the themes of colonization and Victorian stricture by originating a dramatic form that she admits emphasizes the "parallels between the way colonizers treat the colonized and the way men tended to treat women in our society" (1994, 88). Referring to what Genet calls "the colonial or feminine mentality of interiorised repression," Churchill sets the first act of *Cloud Nine* firmly within Victorian, colonized Africa in 1879 and the second in London one hundred years later, with characters inexplicably having aged only twenty-five years. Because colonial Africa had remained virtually into the 1950s, just prior to independence, Churchill is obviously incorporating anachronism for postmodern experimentation rather than historical purposes. This juxtaposition of periods alone, without transitions or narrative explanation, thwarts audience expectations and undermines narrative suspense, especially since act 1 ends with a "cliffhanger" that is never resolved: one of the major characters, Clive, is about to be shot by his servant Joshua. This potential murder, however, is never carried through to its logical conclusion. In fact, act 2 ignores the violent effort completely: although Clive is not specifically a character in the second act, his family refers to him as alive and well. The second act, in other words, depends very little on the first in terms of character development or narrative through-lines.

There is a method to Churchill's madness, however, elucidated more clearly if we examine *Cloud Nine* in the light of one of Russia's most famous theorists and cinematic geniuses, formalist Sergei Eisenstein. Emphasizing the significance of editing or montage as the guiding principle in cinema, Eisenstein believed that "conflict lies at the basis of every art" (1999, 21). For the formalist, juxtaposing one shot, without transition, with another of varying, even opposing strength, appearance, or rhythm created a conflict between a thesis (shot A) and an antithesis (shot B); in other words, only by placing the thesis directly beside its antithesis could true art be revealed. Ultimately, audiences of Eisensteinian montage were forced to resolve this visual collision of opposites individually by creating synthesis, resolving the conflicts between the shots with a new reality, one bred from conflict.

Even with her initial concept in *Cloud Nine*—setting up an act 1 that has very little to do with act 2 in terms of reality, space, time, or cause and effect—Churchill is asking her audiences to create meaning from the juxtapositions of opposites. Austin Quigley explains that "the play does not present the first act as a norm that the second act must follow; nor does it present the first act as a problem to which the second is the solution" (1989, 36). Unlike most playwrights of traditional drama, Churchill is not interested in using act 2 to resolve the conflicts of act

1. She ignores the conventional emphasis on rising action, conflict, falling action, and denouement. Instead, like Eisenstein she challenges her audience to discover that the associations between these two acts are not based on context, character, or even diegesis. Rather, the parallels between the two acts serve completely literary and thematic ends, emphasizing what semiotician Robert Scholes would call the "literariness" or theatricality of the piece without worrying about its basis in reality. In other words, Churchill, imitating Eisenstein's commitment to a collision in style and presentation, not of subject matter, dares her viewers to create meaning even while her text seemingly denies it.

This temporal and spatial disjunctiveness is not the only confusing aspect between the two acts; differing styles also initially deny meaning and create conflict. In act 1 Churchill incorporates broad physical farce to make audiences laugh at the damning relationships between genders and among races in Great Britain. Characters speak in clichés, often relying on conventions of melodrama to express emotions, hide truths, or define gender. For example, when Betty finds herself alone with adventurer Harry Bagley, the two discuss their mutual attraction in comic, unrealistic dialogue:

> BETTY. When I'm near you it's like going out into the jungle. It's like going up the river on a raft. It's like going out in the dark.
> HARRY. And you are safety and light and peace and home.
> BETTY. But I want to be dangerous.
> HARRY. Clive is my friend.
> BETTY. I am your friend.
> HARRY. I don't like dangerous women.
> BETTY. Is Mrs. Saunders dangerous?
> HARRY. Not to me. She's a bit of an old boot.
> BETTY. Am I dangerous?
> HARRY. You are rather.
> BETTY. Please like me.
> HARRY. I worship you.
> BETTY. Please want me.
> HARRY. I don't want to want you. Of course I want you.
> BETTY. What are we going to do?
> HARRY. I should have stayed on the river. The hell with it.
> *He goes to take her in his arms, she runs away into the house.* (Churchill 1994, 14)

Such dialogue reads almost like nineteenth-century melodrama, where the surreptitious lovers exclaim their affection in hyperbolic terms; and the stage directions, heightening Betty's delicacy and piety, also are exaggerated for comic effect, undermining any honest emotion she may be experiencing.

But in act 2 Churchill relies more on traditional, realistic, even cryptic dramatic exchanges, abandoning the farcical elements of the first act almost altogether. This is illustrated by an early conversation between Victoria, now a mother, and Lin, a woman she meets in the park:

LIN. And your husband? How do you get on with him?
VICTORIA. Oh fine. Up and down. You know. Very well. He helps with the washing up and everything.
LIN. I left mine two years ago. He let me keep Cathy and I'm grateful for that.
VICTORIA. You shouldn't be grateful.
LIN. I'm a lesbian.
VICTORIA. You still shouldn't be grateful.
LIN. I'm grateful he didn't hit me harder than he did.
VICTORIA. I suppose I'm lucky with Martin. (Churchill 1994, 51)

Not only is the dialogue in act 2 increasingly realistic, but characters also examine difficult subjects such as war, homosexuality, marital infidelity, and battery in a direct, even confrontational, manner. Churchill introduces similar concepts in act 1, witnessed in Clive's mistreatment of Betty and Mrs. Sanders and his negligent parenting of Edward, but the tone here is essentially manic. In other words, act 1 asks audiences to laugh first and discover innuendoes later; act 2 forces them to confront the realism and violence of subjects such as marital infidelity and battery immediately, as illustrated by Lin's honest admission of her husband's violent behavior or Gerry's insensitive behavior with Edward, certainly diametrically opposed in style and presentation to the jaunty banter of the characters in act 1.

Irving Wardle, in his review of an early London production, exhibits some irritation with this shift in stylistic approaches between acts: "I think Miss Churchill disregards the crude facts of audience psychology by starting the evening with some uproariously coarse jokes at the expense of Victorian pieties, and then modulating into something altogether gentler and non-satirical. Long into last night's second half, here were uneasy giggles from spectators trying to view a study in sexual evolution as if it were another ludicrous chapter in the history of the White Man's Burden" (Wardle 1980). But it is exactly this seemingly unwarranted distinctiveness in style and spatial/temporal dislocation that Churchill uses to create meaning. She gives two thematic reasons for this shift:

The second act is set in London in 1979—this is where I wanted the play to end up, in the changing sexuality of our own time. . . . I felt that the first act would be stronger set in Victorian times, at the height of colonialism, rather than in Africa during the 1950's. And when the company

> talked about their childhood and the attitudes to sex and marriage that
> they had been given when they were very young, everyone felt that they
> had received very conventional, almost Victorian expectations and that
> they had made great changes and discoveries in their lifetimes. (Churchill
> 1994, 89)

So, thematically, this juxtaposition of opposites suggests that, although
the strictures and pieties of Victorian, colonized Africa may be farcical
by contemporary standards, the sexual and gender freedom of London
in 1979 may be even more confusing and less satisfying. In fact, the
characters in 1979 who are free of the strictures imposed by a Victorian
society are not happier, more stable, or even healthier.

In terms of style, however, the shift in time periods is more sophisticated. It forces audiences to forge connections between what they may
have learned as children and what they practice as adults. In other words,
such juxtaposition, which dislocates audiences temporally and spatially,
forces them to see the past and present simultaneously and hints at the
future—all without a firm diegetic context. Furthermore, this leap
in time period from one style to another suggests that true change,
especially in terms of behavior, is almost impossible: characters such as
Edward and Victoria seem destined to repeat learned behavior, even if
they have the best of intentions and strong desires to initiate change.
But Churchill does not stop here.

Instead, within each act she bends gender, asking some actors to shift
genders and leaving others to depict gender realistically. Opening the
show with a musical parody tribute to Great Britain, all seven characters
sing comically and in rhyme the reasons for these shifts in gender. Betty,
played by a man, sings, "I live for Clive. The whole aim of my life / Is
to be what he looks for in a wife. / I am man's creation as you see, /
And what men want is what I want to be" (Churchill 1994, 1). Joshua,
the black servant played by a white actor, announces, "My skin is black
but oh my soul is white / I hate my tribe. My master is my light. / I
only live for him. As you can see, / What white men want is what I
want to be" (2). Like Betty, Clive's son Edward is also played by a
woman ("What father wants I'd dearly like to be / I find it rather hard
as you can see") and his daughter, Victoria, by a dummy (2).

On a surface level such gender-bending antics help to create the farcical, even Monty Pythonesque, tone of the first act, eliciting laughs
from the awkward feminine tossing of a ball to the rough treatment
of Victoria, a doll that is often thrown around like an object, illustrat-
ing her lack of significance in a patriarchal society, especially compared
to her brother. But switching genders also serves a purpose microcos-
mically imitative of the overall montage structure of the play. Having

Betty played by a man, for example, creates tension for audience members and other actors, once again resembling Eisenstein's emphasis on montage within a single shot: "Conflicts that are waiting only for a single intensifying impulse to break up into antagonistic pairs of fragments. Close-ups and long shots. Fragments travelling graphically in different directions. Fragments resolved in volumes and fragments solved in plans. Fragments of darkness and light" (Eisenstein 1999, 22). Like Eisenstein, Churchill asks audiences and other actors onstage to accept the actress who plays Betty as a man, the actress who plays Edward as a boy, the white man who plays Joshua as an African, and the dummy who plays Victoria as a human. Not only must audiences suspend disbelief in an effort to process the sexual advances and narrative developments onstage, but they must also work to synthesize each character individually, making sense of the role reversals within the context of the play, the period, the characters, and the associations between characters.

The semiotic system that Churchill incorporates in act 1 actually works against audiences' achieving synthesis in a conventional manner, especially when compared to act 2. The characters in act 1 are represented, as the initial song indicates, by their "true selves," or how their behavior is read by the dominant culture at the time. Tension here lies within juxtaposing the appearance of a black character such as Joshua with his repressed self, implied by the fact that he is played by a white actor. This distinction between appearance and repressed self, also true with the "gender bent" characters of Betty and Edward, is a guiding code, signaling that people and situations are not what they seem. Churchill suggests, in other words, that we look at the layers underneath to uncover truth. In act 2, with the exception of the character of Cathy (who is played by a man), audiences must look between the lines of the dialogue, not to a gender-bending device, to recognize this distinction between appearance and repression. Martin, for example, subtly exhibits his repressed hostility toward women in a speech supposedly favoring female experimentation:

> You're the one who's experimenting with bisexuality and I don't stop you, I think women have something to give each other. You seem to need the mutual support. You find me too overwhelming. So follow it through, go away, leave me and Tommy alone for a bit, we can manage perfectly well without you. I'm not putting any pressure on you but I don't think you're being a whole person. God knows I do everything I can to make you stand on your own two feet. Just be yourself. You don't seem to realize how insulting it is to me that you can't get yourself together. (Churchill 1994, 72)

Martin honestly believes he is being generous and gentle with Victoria, that his allowance and even encouragement of her bisexuality represents his concern and affection; but his passive/aggressive references to how her behavior reflects on him illustrate that he cares more for himself than he does for her. Whereas audiences in act 1 must look past clothing and appearances to recognize repression, in act 2 they must look between the lines of sophisticated and complex dialogue.

These varied and distinct challenges—to understand the relationship between act 1 and 2 and to process the gender confusion between characters—are ultimately more complex than the deceptively simple action onstage. For example, Churchill examines levels of violence in *Cloud Nine* throughout both acts without ever referring directly to violence onstage. In fact, most of the violence is implicit, occurring offstage or in conversation, so the complexity lies not in the onstage depiction of violence but in its implication.

The most traditional threat of violence in act 1 is from African natives, described by Joshua, who recounts a harrowing tale of his parents' demise, and by adventurer Harry Bagley, who comes to protect the family from the possibility of advancing natives. Sexual violence is an even more prevalent aspect, as evidenced by Bagley's sexually abusive relationship with young Edward or his exploitation of servant Joshua, each referred to onstage but occurring off. Although Clive does take sexual advantage of Mrs. Saunders in the first act, not until the second do characters actually speak in length about sexual confusion. Even the attempt to conduct sexual relationships explicitly in view of the audience is thwarted. For example, the orgy among Lin, Victoria, and Edward is interrupted by the appearance of Lin's dead brother, the soldier, Bill. Only at the end of act 1 is violence onstage ever threatened directly, and even then it is not finally recounted onstage: "While CLIVE is speaking, JOSHUA raises his gun to shoot him. Only EDWARD sees. He does nothing to warn the others. He puts his hands over his ears. BLACK" (Churchill 1994, 47). Because nothing ever comes of this potential "murder," *Cloud Nine* ultimately even denies spectators a narrative depiction of violence, forcing them to imagine the actions behind the scenes as written in order to synthesize the illogical in terms of character, gender, time, space, and causal effect.

The implicit postmodern textual challenges that Churchill forces on her audiences become even more apparent in the second act of *Cloud Nine,* when Churchill asks actors to shift roles. Not one actor plays the same character in act 1 and act 2. All of them are twenty-five years older, and many new characters are introduced. This doubling creates a tension even more directly attributable to Eisenstein's thesis/antithesis theory of montage. Audiences must learn to recognize an old character from act 1 (Betty, for example) played in act 2 by a new actor (the female who played Edward in act 1). Often, Churchill even arranges pairings that illustrate a true character shift, such as asking the actor who portrays the patriarchal Clive in act 1 to play four-year-old Cathy in act 2 (the only gender bending in this act). In the original doubling, the actor Clive plays Cathy; the actor Betty, her son Edward; the actress Edward, his mother Betty; the actress Maud, her granddaughter Victoria; the actress Mrs. Saunders/Ellen, Cathy's lesbian mother Lin; the white actor Joshua, Edward's homosexual love interest Gerry, and the actor Harry, Victoria's feminist husband Martin—all roles quite different at first glance from the original part. Understandably, it takes audiences several minutes to understand who is playing whom, the result of an intentional effort to confuse audiences, which Eisenstein, who likens montage to physics, would have appreciated. "Remember," he maintained, "that physics is aware of an infinite number of combinations arising from the impact (collision) between spheres" (1999, 21). Eisenstein would also have admired Churchill for this doubling, which, like montage, forces audiences to accept one actor in two disparate roles (related only by thematic concerns that sometimes bring the outward and the repressed selves together), much like the conflict he himself inspired within individual shots.

Churchill's effort, of course, is an attempt to make the form of the play analogous to its meaning. As she explains, "The first act, like the society it shows, is male dominated and firmly structured. In the second act, more energy comes from the women and the gays. The uncertainties and changes of society, and more feminine and less authoritarian feeling, are reflected in the looser structure of the act" (Churchill 1994, 89). Ironically, in the one hundred years of "progress" her play represents, Churchill paints a world that seems more accepting of untraditional sexual behavior and more encouraging in its liberal push to help women "find themselves." But the depressing depiction of this new society, and even the second act's lack of overt comic energy, suggests that Churchill remains unconvinced that contemporary life offers easier solutions than its Victorian ancestors. In a world without the strictures of Victorian culture, which were certainly both repressive and oppressive, characters appear lost in the freedom of their seemingly increased cultural awareness.

In her efforts to pursue her rights as a feminist and lesbian, for example, Lin aggressively pursues a relationship with the confused and unhappy Victoria, sometimes ignoring her daughter, Cathy, and often teaching her to be as conventionally aggressive as men by buying her guns and encouraging violence. In scene 2 of act 2 she even strikes Cathy when her daughter refuses to go to bed when asked. Interested finally in achieving the self-fulfillment she cannot find in her marriage, Victoria leaves her son Tommy with her husband to live with Lin and her brother, Edward. At one point she attempts to invoke the spirit of a priestess during the middle of an orgy with the both of them in an effort to discover her true self. Her husband, Martin, tries to understand her needs, even to the point of encouraging Victoria to experiment with other women if she needs to find herself, but ultimately he seems to care more about his own personal and sexual needs than those of his wife or his son.

Victoria's brother, Edward, lives in fear of his lover Gerry's abandoning him, which eventually becomes a self-fulfilling prophecy, and her mother, Betty, must find solace, after she leaves her husband, Clive, in masturbation:

> And one night in my flat I was so frightened I started touching myself. I thought my hand might go through space. I touched my face, it was there, my arm, my breast, and my hand went down where I thought it shouldn't, and I thought well there is somebody there. It felt very sweet . . . . Afterwards I thought I had betrayed Clive. My mother would kill me. But I felt triumphant because I was a separate person from them. And I cried because I didn't want it to be. But I don't cry about it anymore. Sometimes I do it three times in one night and it really is great fun. (Churchill 1994, 82–83)

And even though Churchill paints this newfound ability to masturbate as a true sign of growth and self-acceptance for Betty, it is certainly a bittersweet triumph at best. In fact, it can almost be read as tragic that the one character who seems to mature does so by establishing ties to no one in the play but herself. Finally meeting the Betty from act 1, she hugs her former self to conclude the play.

In his article "Beyond the Shot: The Cinematographic Principle and the Ideogram," Eisenstein defines his theories of collision by applying cinema to other art forms, such as haiku, tanka, the hieroglyph, even Kabuki theatre, and in an article about D. W. Griffith and Charles Dickens he attributes some of his ideas about editing to the parallel montage sequences of early Griffith or the montage style of Dickens in novels such as *Oliver Twist*. Although I have no idea whether Churchill was a student of Eisenstein's theories, or even a fan of his films, her postmodern experiments with time and space in *Cloud Nine* illustrate similar principles of conflict, collision, and art. Her juxtaposition of periods between acts 1 and 2, her efforts to bend gender as far as it logically can be bent, and her use of doubling are all techniques that, when compared to cinema, indicate a play that stylistically sets itself firmly at or outside the margins. Like Eisenstein, Churchill forces audiences to work for meaning and to decipher the nature of truth through the juxtapositions of opposites. It is indeed this experimentation that pushes audiences beyond the words to understand the complexities and paradoxes of the twenty-first century.

Works Cited

Churchill, Caryl. *Cloud Nine*. 1994. New York: Theatre Communications Group.

Eisenstein, Sergei. 1999. "Beyond the Shot: The Cinematographic Principle and the Ideogram." Reprint. In *Film Theory and Criticism*, ed. Leo Braudy and Marshall Cohen. New York: Oxford University Press.

Quigley, Austin. 1989. "Stereotype and Prototype: Character in the Plays of Caryl Churchill." In *Feminine Focus*, ed. Enoch Brater. New York: Oxford University Press.

Wardle, Irving. 1980. "Review of *Cloud Nine*." *Times* (London), 10 September, p. 10.

Cadences of Cruelty

Artaud's Discursive Performance

Robert I. Lublin

This spectacle is more than we can assimilate, assailing us with a super-abundance of impressions, each richer than the next, but in a language to which it seems we no longer have the key; and this kind of irritation created by the impossibility of finding the thread and tracking the beast down—the impossibility of putting one's ear closer to the instrument in order to hear better—is one charm the more to the credit of this spectacle.

—Artaud 1958

In the Zohar, the story of Rabbi Simeon who burns like fire is as immediate as fire itself.

—Artaud 1958

CONCEIVED IN THE FIERY WORKINGS of a sickened mind and riddled with paradox, Antonin Artaud's conceptualization of a theatre of cruelty seems virtually impossible to achieve onstage. And yet the writings that detail this "impossible" theatre proved tremendously influential in the 1960s, and critical interest in Artaud has not diminished since but actually seems to be growing (Finter 1997, 18). What could explain the appeal of critical works that are all but defined by contradiction and fraught with erroneous statements? The answer lies in Artaud's powers of artistic creation. Artaud was equally comfortable writing plays and poetry as he was theorizing about drama, and his vision of a theatre of cruelty was not elaborated in a straightforward, prescriptive manner but in a complex, dramatic voice. As a result his essays have a dual existence—as explanations of Artaud's theatre and as performative events in their own right. In this bifurcated capacity Artaud's works serve to forward his theoretical agenda through the discursive execution of the strategies of the theatre of cruelty that they were written to describe. Thus, although the creation of a full-fledged theatre of cruelty is unlikely, its vitality and immediacy, as evidenced in Artaud's essays, can be felt as a viable force.

Only in such a dramatic discursive strategy can a quote such as that from "On the Balinese Theater," which began this essay, serve any critical objective. Otherwise, its meaning quickly dissolves under examination. To begin with, we know that Artaud was unfamiliar with the language and customs of the Balinese he described in his essay. Consequently, the fact that their performance demonstrates a language of impressions to which "we no longer have a key" connotes ignorance in the observer as much as it suggests great wisdom in the performer. And because the semiotic system of the Balinese was unknown to Artaud, it similarly follows that the "superabundance of impressions, each richer than the next," was not necessarily inherent to the Balinese theatre but is more likely projected on the performance by the unknowledgeable spectator.

However, Artaud never intended his works to be read in this manner. In the same way that he repudiates realistic, psychological theatre, Artaud eschews straightforward, prescriptive writing strategies. Both are inadequate for conveying information to an audience. Artaud asserts that "words say little to the mind; extent and objects speak; new images speak, even new images made with words" (1958, 87). Although these remarks were meant to describe the use of dialogue onstage, they prove equally valid for words on the page. In his essays Artaud uses language not to simply explain or convey but to create images that will violently assault the reader. In this manner Artaud's written page becomes the site of the theatre of cruelty.

Accordingly, the dubious aspects of "On the Balinese Theater" disappear in the world of images designed to assault his reader that Artaud creates in his essay. Like Artaud watching the Balinese performance, we read his essay and are "irritated and charmed" by the inability to fully understand the force of this foreign performance. We seek meaning, "tracking the beast down," but all that we are able to get are impressions—impressions overwhelmingly powerful and too great to be fully assimilated. Furthermore, these impressions are spoken in a language to which we "no longer have the key." In this manner Artaud hints at a greater world to which we should aspire both in our art and in our lives.

This greater world, Artaud suggests, is one with which we have lost all communion but that remains alive and thriving in the spectacles of the Balinese: "In a spectacle like that of Balinese theater there is something that has nothing to do with entertainment, the notion of useless, artificial amusement, of an evening's pastime which is the characteristic of our theater. The Balinese productions take shape at the very heart of matter, life, reality" (1958, 60).

Artaud's appreciation for the Balinese theatre is unmediated; he finds it superior to the Occidental theatre in every way. However, since we know that Artaud had little understanding of Balinese society or performance, this disposition necessarily tells us more about his own society's theatre than that of the Other on which he lavishes so much praise. Therefore, rather than demonstrating an unmediated appreciation for the Balinese theatre, Artaud instead succeeds primarily in highlighting his unmediated disgust for the Occidental theatre. He states that the Balinese actors "make an exact quantity of specific gestures, of well-tried mime at a given point, and above all in the prevailing spiritual tone, the deep and subtle study that has presided at the elaboration of these plays of expression, these powerful signs which give us the impression that their power has not weakened during thousands of years" (1958, 55). Although Artaud records his dissatisfaction with Occidental, psychological acting throughout his essays, here he brings it to life, highlighting its weaknesses by detailing the success of its opposite. The Balinese theatre deals in gestures that have retained their power for thousands of years, whereas the Occidental theatre is effete, having long ago lost its power to communicate. Similarly, where the Balinese theatre is noted for its spiritual tone, the Occidental theatre dissatisfies because of its adherence to a banal realism.

But Artaud accomplishes far more in his essay "On the Balinese Theater" than merely chastising the Parisian theatre. He recreates the Balinese theatre as he saw it. However, as James Elkins explains, even "'objective' descriptions are permeated, soaked, with . . . unspoken, unthought desires" (1996, 33). To Artaud the Balinese theatre constituted the essential Other he had been seeking with all of his creative endeavors but had not been able to find. In the cryptic performance of the Balinese theatre that he saw at the Colonial Exposition in the summer of 1931, Artaud found a creative space that he could fill with his own generative desires. As a result, "On the Balinese Theater" is a distinctively Artaudian creation. Nevertheless, it maintains a tight connection with the Balinese theatre by claiming to describe it. By being associated with an actual performance, Artaud's essay gains a legitimacy that wholly theoretical examinations of the theatre inevitably lack. Artaud's discussion may seem vague, overwhelming, and literally incredible; but it is also, in a manner, undeniable and can be validated simply by situating it on a specific date and at a particular time, the date and place of the original performance. Artaud preemptively refutes any suggestion that this theatre is unachievable by stating that "of this idea of pure theater, which is merely theoretical in the Occident and to which no one has ever attempted to give the least reality, the Balinese offer us a stupefying realization" (1958, 61).

Because "On the Balinese Theater" details an Artaudian performance (i.e., a "product" of his mind), it deserves examination. Furthermore, in a moment of self-reflection in the middle of the essay, Artaud admits to the subjectivity of the work. While discussing the Balinese use of stage space and gesture on a metaphysical level, suddenly and without explanation he interjects his own identity, writing, "[A]t least that is the way they appear to us" (1958, 61). The sudden introduction of the subjective viewer seems not only odd but contradictory in light of the ostensibly universal messages of the performance. Bettina Knapp offers a possible explanation for Artaud's insertion of self: "His physical and mental torment was so acute as to make it impossible for him to see the world except through the dark prism of his tortured Self" (1969, 198). Another explanation, however, can be found in the effect of such a writing strategy on a reader.

By referring to himself in the first-person plural, Artaud places his reader alongside him in viewing this production. The performance being viewed, however, is Artaud's. Sitting beside us, commenting on the play and simultaneously creating the conditions of its performance, Artaud has assumed a powerful authorial position from which to articulate his concept of a new theatre. This authority in the text mirrors the importance of the director in Artaud's theatre.

One of the most significant changes Artaud wanted to effect in the theatre was to shift the focus from the text to the performance. Toward this end he advocated a theatre that had no written text or, if there were one, a text that would provide only the barest bones of the performance. Instead, the unifying force in a production would be the director, to whom would be ceded all responsibilities formerly belonging to both the playwright and the scene designer. With all of this power, the director would have singular control over the performance, and the actors would be responsible for realizing his or her vision. The director in Artaud's theatre would be a creator-god (Bermel 1977, 29). When we consider this one, concrete element of Artaud's theatre, the written performance of Artaud's theatre of cruelty might be said to surpass its dramatic presentation. Artaud's published works can be received by their audience unmediated by the influences of other artists such as are required to produce a play in the theatre.[1]

---

[1] Artaud once complained that the failure of *Les Cenci*, his one attempt at realizing a theatre of cruelty, was due in part to the unwillingness of the actors to accept his complete control (Costich 1978, 49).

Naturally, in writing about a "pure" performance such as that which he found in the Balinese theatre, Artaud encounters no such problems: "The Balinese have realized, with the utmost rigor, the idea of pure theater, where everything, conception and realization alike, has value, has existence only in proportion to its degree of objectification on the stage. They victoriously demonstrate the absolute preponderance of the director (metteur en scène) whose creative power eliminates words" (1958, 53–54). Like the director who has absolute preponderance in the Balinese theatre, Artaud is the author who has absolute preponderance over the text. In his discursive performance, Artaud is able to go beyond merely attempting to control the actions of actors; through writing he tries to directly influence his audience by creating the action directly in their minds.

Ironically, Artaud achieves this authority and power in essays that frequently assert the inadequacy of words. Indeed, in this essay and throughout *The Theater and Its Double* Artaud actively repudiates spoken language for its inability to affect an audience; he seeks a theatre with the creative power to "eliminate words." Without the hindrance of speech, he argues, theatre would be able to use images, gestures, and sound to transcend the intellectual and impact an audience at the visceral level. Naturally, this is difficult to accomplish in an essay, where words provide the only means of communicating with one's audience.

But Artaud surmounts the inadequacy of language by using words for more than their ordinary semantic designation in order to provide his audience with the experience that he finds superior to speech. Utilizing unusual combinations of rarely connected concepts without concern for contradiction, Artaud manipulates language in an attempt to transcend its limitations. In Bakhtinian terms Artaud thoroughly employs the dialogic potential of language by separating the words from their familiar contexts and forcing the reader to engage the words (Bakhtin 1981, 277). Once words (or in this case, a monologic voice) have been removed from a performance, one begins to speak in an ancient language that is not limited by the stagnancy (overrepetition) typical of the Occidental world. In this manner Artaud is not trying to create, but rather to liberate, a theatre of gestures. His essay thus tries to sweep away the dead aspects of theatre and recreate its vital experience for his audience again for the first time:

> What is in fact curious about all these gestures, these angular and abruptly abandoned attitudes, these syncopated modulations formed at the back of the throat, these musical phrases that break off short, these flights of elytra, these rustlings of branches, these sounds of hollow drums, these robot squeakings, these dances of animated manikins, is this: that through

the labyrinth of their gestures, attitudes, and sudden cries, through the gyrations and turns which leave no portion of the stage space unutilized, the sense of a new physical language, based upon signs and no longer upon words, is liberated. (1958, 54)

Reading this quotation affords little insight into what Artaud actually saw when he watched the Balinese theatre. Rather, the reader receives *impressions* of various sounds and motions that have never before been juxtaposed. We start with the body's assuming attitudes that it quickly abandons in favor of others. Next, we have sounds made with the back of the throat, a place normally reserved for guttural utterances. Then, there are bits of music, but these are broken off and thus deprived of any coherent denotation. Finally, we are "thrust into bewilderment" by a series of sounds and movements—flights of elytra, rustlings of branches, sounds of hollow drums, robot squeakings, and dances of animated manikins—that are alien to our typical theatre experience. In our effort to combine such disparate, confusing, and alien elements into a single experience (as Artaud assures us they were presented by the Balinese), we begin to experience, in our minds, the conditions of a theatre of cruelty.

Artaud carries this experience one step further toward fulfilling his theoretical agenda by adding a metaphysical commentary to his discussion of the Balinese theatre. This is important because Artaud wants his readers to be overwhelmed, not simply confused. He writes that "these spiritual signs have a precise meaning which strikes us only intuitively but with enough violence to make useless any translation into logical discursive language" (1958, 54). In this manner Artaud informs his readers that they have not lost the significance of the essay simply because they cannot reiterate its message in spoken language; the import of Artaud's essay is much greater than mere words can convey.

Once Artaud has brought the Balinese theatre to life through the words of his essay and expounded on its metaphysical significance to the liberation of its audience, he begins the same process again. Using either different words or different combinations of words to signify the same event, Artaud once again assaults his readers with images they can only partially understand: "One of the reasons for our delight in this faultless performance lies precisely in the use these actors make of an exact quantity of specific gestures, of well-tried mime at a given point, and above all in the prevailing spiritual tone, the deep and subtle study that has presided at the elaboration of these plays of expression, these powerful signs which give us the impression that their power has not weakened during thousands of years" (1958, 55). Of course, none of this information is new to the reader, but the perfection of the Balinese theatre has, in Artaud's seemingly repetitive description, been made abundantly clear; the superiority of gesture as communicative agent has been noted; and, finally, the timelessness of gesture has been discussed.

If all of these features have been addressed already, what purpose does it serve to repeat them? The question is moot because Artaud does not, in fact, repeat himself. In changing words or the sentence structures in which they are used, Artaud succeeds not only in addressing the material again but in addressing the material afresh. Through his recursive writing technique, Artaud is able to assault his readers rigorously and continuously, giving them "a superabundance of impressions," all related to a single experience. Furthermore, Artaud does not merely repeat his ideas in different words but effectually alters the form and forcefulness with which he asserts them. In this manner Artaud's essay reads like music, with rising and falling cadences. Thus, when we read "On the Balinese Theater," we are struck by impressions that are hard and soft, fast and slow, concrete and abstract. At one point we read an almost analytical explanation of the multiplicity of senses that are intertwined in the Balinese performance: "And the most commanding interpenetrations join sight to sounds, intellect to sensibility, the gesture of a character to the evocation of a plant's movement across the scream of an instrument" (1910, 35). The same general idea, repeated several paragraphs later, sounds quite different: "This dazzling ensemble full of explosions, flights, secret streams, detours in every direction of both external and internal perception, composes a sovereign idea of the theater" (1958, 59). Rising and falling, swelling and shrinking, Artaud's explanation of the Balinese theatre is a rich elliptical performance that works on the sensibilities of his readers by challenging their ordinary method of engaging a text.

And yet despite the fact that Artaud repeatedly addresses the same performance using different wording and varied styles, we never gain a more concrete understanding of the Balinese performance. Sometimes Artaud acknowledges this aspect of his explanation: "the themes are vague, abstract, extremely general. They are given life only by the fertility and intricacy of all the artifices of the stage" (1958, 54). At other times, however, Artaud suggests that there is a complete world of signs just beyond our reach to which we should be privy and must aspire to understand. "These howls, these rolling eyes," he states, "this continuous abstraction, these noises of branches, noises of the cutting and rolling of wood, all within the immense area of widely diffused sounds disgorged from any sources, combine to overwhelm the mind, to crystallize as a new and, I dare say, concrete conception of the abstract" (1958, 64). It is impossible for a reader to understand this concrete conception of the abstract, but in the effort to embrace its paradox, he or she experiences Artaudian cruelty.

The importance of this aspect of "On the Balinese Theater" is heightened by the fact that it is a constant throughout Artaud's writings. As Susan Sontag has noted, "[D]espite the breaks in exposition and the varying of 'forms' within each work, everything he wrote advances a line of argument" (Artaud 1976, xxv). Thus far, this "argument" has been largely limited to an examination of the performative discursive strategies in "On the Balinese Theater," but it need not have been. I chose this particular essay as my paradigm of Artaud's writing style because it is perhaps the one least examined in *The Theater and Its Double*. The performative nature of Artaud's writing and the issues about which he felt most strongly, however, remain constant throughout his works. Consequently, this examination of "On the Balinese Theater" can be seen as a microcosm of a larger study of Artaud's discursive performance in *The Theater and Its Double*. In such a study the differences noted between the cadences of the various sections of "On the Balinese Theater" would be expanded into an examination of the different cadences present in the individual essays. Such an examination would reveal different approaches and larger variations, but all remain subservient to Artaud's larger agenda of cruelty.

This repetitive writing style was something Artaud was aware of long before he began writing *The Theater and Its Double*. In "All Writing Is Garbage," a 1925 address to those who write "correctly," Artaud admits the "faulty" manner of his writing, claiming, "I always use the same words and really I don't seem to advance very much in my thinking, but actually I am advancing more than you, bearded asses, pertinent pigs, masters of the false word, wrappers of portraits, serial writers, groundlings, cattle raisers, entomologists, plague of my speech" (1976, 86). The elliptical writing patterns to which Artaud alludes are part of an intentional strategy of cruelty through which he attempts to directly engage his reader's sensibilities. Again and again in his work, Artaud returns to the same crucial issues, assaulting his readers (with a formidable string of insults in "All Writing Is Garbage") in the hope of provoking a visceral response.

Because of his confrontational agenda, Artaud quite naturally was drawn to the theatre as an art form. In the theatre one can go beyond mere words and directly assault the body of the audience: "The theater is the only place in the world, the last general means we still possess of directly affecting the organism and, in periods of neurosis and petty sensuality like the one in which we are immersed, of attacking this sensuality by physical means it cannot withstand" (1958, 81). Ideally, Artaud did not want to communicate with his audience verbally; instead, he wanted to shock its spirit through a physical experience in the theatre. He believed that this was not only possible but had already been accomplished by the Orientals: "But by an altogether Oriental means of expression, this objective and concrete language of the theater can fascinate and ensnare the organs. It flows into the sensibility" (91).

The necessity, for Artaud, of direct physical connection between the actors and the audience explains his eventual loathing for movies, which, he says, murder us with their "second-hand reproductions which, filtered through machines, cannot unite with our sensibility" (1958, 84). Out of this desire for direct contact comes Artaud's most comprehensible and specific prescription for the theatre of cruelty: that the audience in his theatre must sit on mobile chairs in the middle of a nondescript room with four walls with the action taking place all around them. Additionally, there must be a central location, ostensibly located in the midst of the audience (Artaud is not very clear on this point), where climaxes in the action can take place (96–97). Artaud's reason for designing his theatre to conform to these parameters is self-evident. He wanted to affect his audience directly by bringing it into close contact with the actors, who would be "swarming over each other like bees" (97). By so doing he anticipated that the performance would engulf everyone present in a shared experience of life: "the action will unfold, will extend its trajectory from level to level, point to point; paroxysms will suddenly burst forth, will flare up like fires in different spots" (97).

Throughout Artaud's writings we find the impulse to explode with energy, an impulse driven by his desire to break free of the confines Artaud felt in the world around him. His most sophisticated development of this concept is found in "The Theater and the Plague." Although this essay was the last one written for *The Theater and Its Double*, it appears first in the book, arguably because it foregrounds Artaud's desire to engage his audience physically and to directly impact their lives.

In "The Theater and the Plague" Artaud argues for an understanding of plague that is essentially positive. The plague, he says, is not merely a destroyer of civilization; it is also a rejuvenator. Once a society has developed to the point that its mores are ossified into unquestioned laws, it is essentially dead. Citizens of such a society live their lives in a daze, quietly and obediently following rules that prevent them from ever having an immediate, unmediated experience with their world. Releasing people from the rules that bind them requires a tremendous force. When plague strikes, this release is effected: "Once the plague is established in a city, the regular forms collapse" (1958, 23).

The fact that this newfound freedom may result in hideous acts (theft, murder, rape, etc.) by people freed from moral governance does not diminish Artaud's optimism at the possibility for genuine life among the living. He fully expects "a social disaster so far-reaching, an organic disorder so mysterious—this overflow of vices, this total exorcism which presses and impels the soul to its utmost—all indicate the presence of a state which is nevertheless characterized by extreme strength and in which all the powers of nature are freshly discovered at the moment when something essential is going to be accomplished" (1958, 27). Artaud therefore not only concedes the possibility of evil being performed once the plague has arrived, but he actually welcomes it. The dark acts that follow the ravage of plague are inextricably linked to the freedom experienced by those who carry them out. As he says, "[A]ll true freedom is dark" (30). The spontaneous connection with the world that the survivors will experience once the plague has drained society of its illusions and self-imposed constrictions is worth any price.

But Artaud does not argue for the creation and release of a plague that will decimate society and leave only a few survivors to genuinely experience life. He does not advocate the wholesale destruction of humanity but, rather, addresses his effort toward humankind's liberation, a liberation that will occur through theatre. The "true theater," as he calls it, is capable of restoring mankind's connection with the world in the same way the plague can: "Like the plague it reforges the chain between what is and what is not, between the virtuality of the possible and what already exists in materialized nature. . . . The theater restores us all our dominant conflicts and all their powers" (27).

But what does the "true theater," one that can have this tremendous impact on its audience, look like? This is the point at which Artaud's theories stumble. Unwilling to write in a straightforward manner, Artaud never provides us with the means to physically realize his theatre. As a result, the finest example we have of a theatre of cruelty is the "performance" that occurs on reading Artaud's essays. Thus, through the course of "The Theater and the Plague" Artaud does not merely *discuss* the nature of a liberating plague, but he assaults our sensibilities with it. In what might appear on first examination a superfluous and overly grotesque explanation of the effects of the plague, Artaud compels his readers to actually *experience* it. He describes the effects of the plague on the body in such detail that he forces his reader to viscerally experience the pain and death that the plague brings with it. Each of the senses is in turn assaulted and overwhelmed by the forces that tear through the body. "The body is covered with red spots . . . [and] his head begins to boil. . . . His crazed body fluids, unsettled and commingled, seem to be flooding through his flesh. . . . [T]he inside of his

stomach seems as if it were trying to gush out between his teeth . . .
aberration of his mind, beating in hurried strokes like his heart, which
grows intense, heavy, loud; his eyes, first inflamed, then glazed . . . his
swollen gasping tongue . . . " (19). Touch, thought, internal organs,
sight, taste, all are engaged by the sickness. In this way Artaud does
not merely discuss the plague that can liberate people from false pre-
tensions but attempts to embody it for the liberation of his readers.

Despite the evocative power of the language of his essays, Artaud
was not content to merely write about theatre, and he continued to
hope until the end of his life that he might realize his theories onstage.
The power of theatre to directly engage an audience was too much for
Artaud to ignore, even after his one attempt at creating a theatre of
cruelty proved largely unsuccessful. In the last extant document from
Artaud, a letter to Paule Thevenin, Artaud writes that "from now on
[I] will devote myself exclusively to the theater as I conceive it, a theater
of blood, a theater which with each performance will have done something bodily to the one who performs as well as to the one who comes
to see others perform" (Artaud 1976, 585). Ironically, despite Artaud's
devotion to the theatre and his unswerving belief in its expressive
power, it is his discursive performances, contained in his essays, that
seem to best capture and reflect his theories of a theatre of cruelty.

Works Cited

Artaud, Antonin. 1958. *The Theater and Its Double*. Trans. Mary Caroline
 Richards. New York: Grove Press.
———. 1976. *Antonin Artaud: Selected Writings*. Ed. Susan Sontag. Trans.
 Helen Weaver. Berkeley: University of California Press.
Bakhtin, Mikhail. 1981. *The Dialogic Imagination: Four Essays*. Ed. Michael
 Holquist. Trans. Caryl Emerson and Michael Holquist. Austin: University of
 Texas Press.
Bermel, Albert. 1977. *Artaud's Theatre of Cruelty*. New York: Taplinger.
Costich, Julia F. 1978. *Antonin Artaud*. Boston: Twayne.
Elkins, James. 1996. *The Object Stares Back*. San Diego: Harcourt Brace.
Finter, Helga. 1997. "Antonin Artaud and the Impossible Theatre: The Legacy
 of the Theatre of Cruelty." *Drama Review* 41 (winter): 15–40.
Knapp, Bettina L. 1969. *Antonin Artaud: Man of Vision*. New York: David
 Lewis.

"A Most Magnificent Shew"

Philadelphia's Grand Federal Procession of 1788

Mark E. Mallett

THROUGHOUT THE EARLY MONTHS OF 1788, cities up and down the Atlantic seaboard hosted a series of public exhibitions quite unlike any in the North American experience. Known collectively as the Federal Processions, they comprised parades; banquets; grand displays of commercial, manufacturing, and agricultural bounty; and representations of local history and heritage. These demonstrations combined elements of holiday festivity, commemoration, and triumphal celebration.[1] Among the many innovative features of the exhibitions, the fact that they were staged all over the country marks a significant turning point in the development of a national culture. Colonial society, after all, had never been especially hospitable to such activity.[2] Since the

---

[1] Descriptions of the Federal Processions are drawn from a variety of contemporary newspapers, including the *Albany Gazette, Hudson Valley Gazette, New York Daily Advertiser, New York Federal Herald, New York Morning Post and Daily Advertiser, New York Packet,* and *New Hampshire Spy.*

[2] There had been some common holidays, like the king's birthday, during the colonial period. Different colonies or regions, however, had their own ways of observing or ignoring general occasions like Christmas. Generally, Puritan New Englanders' calendar observed a mere four festivals; Delaware Valley Quakers abolished both religious holidays and English folk festivals. Only south of the tidewater was festivity a regular feature of the culture, with annual observances tied to both the Christian calendar and natural harvest cycles. All these, furthermore, had their origins in the traditions of British culture,

end of the American War of Independence, Americans had had few occasions for general celebrations.

The Federal Processions differed from prior celebrations. Unlike calendrical holidays or Revolutionary commemoration, for instance, each city held its celebration on a day of its own choosing: Boston, 8 February 1788; Baltimore, 1 May 1788; Charleston, 27 May 1788; Portsmouth, New Hampshire, 26 June 1788. Nor did these celebrations become a fixed part of the American festival repertoire. Despite the uniqueness of such detail, however, an obvious pattern of organization, staging, and intent justifies considering all the celebrations as a single phenomenon. Central to this unity is the common theme of the festivities: celebrating the federation of the previously autonomous states under a new national Constitution. From New England to the Carolinas and Georgia, Americans were creating a national identity as they created a nation.

Earlier studies have examined the constitutional celebrations as singular events or, at most, a unique series of events tied solely to the constitutional ratification campaign. Perhaps the bluntest example of this is Constitution scholar Michael Kammen's dismissive comment that the Federal Processions "combined homage to the new government with a pro-Constitution public relations campaign" (1987, 45). Alfred F. Young and Laura Rigal, on the other hand, provide insightful readings of the federal processions as manifesting an emerging class structure in the American manufacturing system (Young 1984, 181–212; Rigal 1996, 253–78; see also Davis 1986, 117–25; Gilje 1987, 189–90; Wilentz 1983, 37–77). They and others have also noted the strong similarities between the Federal Processions and European and English pageants and festivals such as Royal entries, Triumphs, and London's Lord Mayor's Day celebrations.[3] These similarities are without question remarkable, even more so because they were not part of the colonial tradition (Wiebe 1984, 7–11). Unaddressed, however, are the questions of why the federalist faction chose such a theatrical, not to mention foreign, mode of discourse to argue the cause and how they constructed their unusual productions.

---

having been transplanted at the colonies' foundings. See, for example, Solberg 1977, 230–31; and Fischer 1989, 158–66, 368–71, 560–62. One clear exception was the Puritan festival of Thanksgiving, which dated from at least 1630 or 1631 and had been an annual event since 1676.

[3] See David M. Bergeron, *English Civic Pageantry, 1558–1642* (Columbia: University of South Carolina Press, 1970); and Barbara Wisch and Susan Scott Munshower, eds., *Triumphal Celebrations and the Rituals of Statecraft*, vol. 4 (Philadelphia: Pennsylvania State University Press, 1990).

The indirectness of theatricality may help to explain the first question. The federalist project was highly suspect to much of the polity, and the question of adopting the new Constitution provoked bitterly contentious debate both in state legislatures and in the public at large. As individual states began to ratify the Constitution, antifederalist attacks became increasingly strident, charging the federalists with undoing the accomplishments of the Revolution, especially on matters of personal liberty (Wills 1982, vii–viii). The processions, therefore, were designed to downplay the radical changes the federalist agenda necessarily entailed. Rather, the dramaturgy of the Federal Processions emphasized the unfinished task begun in 1776. The parades were staged to present the Constitution and federalism as an embodiment of the fundamental goals of the Revolution (Davis 1986, 117). Dr. Benjamin Rush, a key federalist theorist and a member of Philadelphia's "Committee of Arrangements," described the effect they hoped to achieve with their performances: "The connection of the great event of independence, the French alliance, the Peace, and the name of General Washington with the adoption of the Constitution was happily calculated to unite the most remarkable of transports of the mind which were felt during the war with the great event of the day, and to produce such a tide of joy as has seldom been felt in any age or country" (Butterfield 1951, 470).

By so weaving together the threads of the Revolution and independence narratives with that of the Constitution, the federalists sought to legitimate what amounted to a second revolution. Underlying the federalist festivals was a deliberate effort to appropriate the public sphere and the rhetoric of performance. In his keynote speech concluding Philadelphia's celebration, James Wilson made this clear as he explained the cultural utility of the Federal Processions: "They may instruct and improve, while they entertain and please. They may point out the elegance or usefulness of the sciences and the arts. They may preserve the memory, and engrave the importance of great political events. They may represent, with peculiar felicity and force, the operations and effects of great political truths" (Hazard 1828, 417).

A desire to avoid direct confrontation no doubt also partially explains why the federalists chose to present their vision of republican culture in the allegorical imagery of the Federal Processions rather than in the logical arguments that they had used for their new government. The visual emphasis of the Federal Processions focused spectators' attention on the physical presentation. In this way the federalists were able to employ a symbolic vocabulary that deferred specific vocalization of their cultural ideology while it sustained popular enthusiasm for the principal institution of that ideology.

An examination of federalist writings shows clearly that they understood and intended their processions to be theatre, in terms of both form and function. In his January 1787 "Address to the People of the United States," Rush chided his fellow Americans for having failed to realize the promise of the Revolution: "[T]he war is over: but this is far from the case with the American Revolution. On the contrary, nothing but the first act of the great drama is closed. It remains yet to establish and perfect our new forms of government, and to prepare the principles, morals and manners of our citizens for those forms of government after they are established and brought to perfection."[4]

Dr. Rush's reproach was couched in terms that his fellow patriots, at least, could not misapprehend. Playhouse metaphors had figured prominently in the rhetoric of independence before the war and still retained much of their pre-Revolution potency. Each occurrence invoked a powerful image of America as the performance of a divine play before an audience of nations and before God, all of whom would sit in judgment. George Washington had stated the idea forcefully in a 1783 letter to the new states' governors. Americans, he wrote, having secured independence, "are from this period to be considered as actors on a most conspicuous Theatre, which seems to be peculiarly designed by Providence for the display of human greatness and felicity" (quoted in Richards 1991, 36).

Rush's reference to the "great drama" was not simply a rhetorical flourish, though. It was also a rejoinder to what he and many federalists perceived as a widespread complacency that was dangerously undermining completion of the Americans' nation-building task. To their way of thinking, the "Revolution" was far greater than the war for independence or even independence itself. Rather, as John Adams later argued in a letter to Thomas Jefferson, the war "was no part of the Revolution; it was only an effect and a consequence of it. The Revolution was in the minds of the people, and this was effected, from 1760 to 1775, in the course of fifteen years before a drop of blood was shed at Lexington" (quoted in Howard 1989, 82).

Four months earlier, in September 1786, delegates from five states had met in Annapolis to petition the sitting Congress to consider a practical national Constitution. Another four months passed between Rush's address and the Constitutional Convention that met in May 1787 in Phila-

---

[4]Rush had earlier shared these ideas with his friend Richard Price in a letter dated 25 May 1786: "This [the end of the revolution] is so far from being the case that we have only finished the first act of the great drama. . . . [I]t remains yet to effect a revolution in our principles, opinions, and manners so as to accommodate them to the forms of government we have adopted" (quoted in Butterfield 1951, 388).

delphia. Finally, in September 1787 that body concluded its work and sent the new Constitution of the United States to the thirteen state legislatures for ratification. Within this context, Jeffrey Richards notes, "Rush's refiguration [insisted that] the drama had not ended at all; there are still four acts left." Furthermore, this refiguration "has a distinct advantage of keeping before the public a familiar image of progress . . . while it restarts the clock of expectation" (Richards 1991, 281).

Equally important, Rush displaced the war from its symbolic primacy as the embodiment of the revolution. From the federalist perspective, independence was but the first step toward realizing a better society. The promise of such a society had been an essential theme of the Revolution and had animated the colonists' prosecution of the war. Thomas Paine's influential prewar pamphlet, *Common Sense,* stated it boldly: "We have it in our power to begin the world over again. A similar situation to the present has not happened since the day of Noah until now. The Birthday of a new world is at hand" (quoted in Kramnick and Foot 1987, 23).

Fulfillment of the promise of that revolution was now in peril thanks in no small part to a general conflation of the war with the drama. This equation arose not simply out of war weariness; it was also commonly expressed at the end of the war by the leading military (hence, nationally prominent) figures. "The play is over," wrote Lafayette after the surrender at Yorktown, "the fifth act has just ended" (1781, 422). Washington himself seemed to confirm it a year and a half later in his farewell address to his troops: "Nothing now remains but for the actors of this mighty scene to preserve a perfect unvarying consistency of character to the very last act, to close the drama with applause; and to retire from the military Theatre" (quoted in Albanese 1976, 106). Rush's refiguration thus opened a rhetorical space in which the revolution's synecdochal boundaries could expand to include the cultural shifts that had anticipated the war.

Nor was Rush's choice of image limited to metonymy. It was also a strategic invocation of the transformative potential that had arisen in the performance of the "great drama's" first act. Rush had witnessed firsthand the success with which patriot radicals in New England had turned popular rituals of regulation and punishment into performances of political protest (Fearnow 1992, 53–64; Young 1984, 185–212). Anticipating antifederal resistance, Rush was reaching back to the imagery and the unity that had so effectively sustained the patriots' cause up to and throughout the war. By pushing back the final curtain, Rush hoped to infuse the projects of his remaining "acts" with, and so connect them to, a pre-Revolutionary zeal.

Prior to the adoption of the Constitution, these celebrations were associated with the ratification of individual states. As approval grew imminent, however, federalist leaders began to prepare for a national celebration in Philadelphia. When Congress, then seated in Philadelphia, confirmed the Constitution's adoption on 2 July 1788, Pennsylvania's ratification celebrations were combined with Fourth of July ceremonies. In many ways the Philadelphians also celebrated for the entire nation.

The Philadelphia festival featured centrally a monumental parade, or "Grand Federal Procession," through the main streets of the city, and the celebration concluded with a huge public banquet. Approximately five thousand marchers, stretching more than a mile and a half, formed for the parade, which took more than three hours to progress along a three-mile course from Third Street to "the Union Green," the "spacious lawn" of a prominent private estate (Beer 1993, 361–63).

Participants had begun assembling around eight o'clock that morning. Church bells announced the special day to the city, and the ship *Rising Sun*—"anchored off Market Street, and superbly decorated" (Hazard 1828, 417)—fired a salute from the harbor. Philadelphians turned out by the thousands to watch the parade, adding to the marvel of the day. One federalist observer wrote with pride that all along the parade route "the footways, the windows, and roofs of the houses were crowded with spectators, exhibiting a spectacle truly magnificent and irresistibly animating" (Rush 1788, 75–76).

The parade stepped off around 9:30, led by twelve "axe-men" dressed in pioneer hunting frocks, followed by a troop of light dragoons escorting a body of marchers and riders. Many in this body carried flags emblazoned with images and labels commemorating, variously, "Fourth of July 1776," Independence, the states' ratification conventions, General Washington, the peace treaty, and "a new aera" (Hazard 1828, 417–425; Bell 1962, 5–39).[5] Near the end of this first detachment of the parade marched a group of soldiers. A band of musicians playing a new "Federal March," written especially for the occasion, brought up the rear (Silverman 1987, 532).

The musicians' new melody heralded several innovative parade elements, at least on the American scene. As they passed, a light blue carriage, twenty feet long and drawn by six white horses, rolled along on huge wheels (those at the rear were eight feet in diameter), bearing a framed copy of the new Constitution over the words *THE PEOPLE*. The carriage's centerpiece was a "lofty, ornamental car" in the form of a large bald eagle, "thirteen feet high . . . thirteen feet long . . . emblazoned with thirteen stars in a sky-blue field." The car was draped with

---

[5]See also Davis 1986, 117–25; Silverman 1987, 583–87; and Young 1984, 200–204.

a banner that read "THE CONSTITUTION" and carried three judges "in their robes of office." The whole display was decorated with liberty caps (Hazard 1828, 418).

Francis Hopkinson, a principal planner of the Grand Federal Procession, marched immediately behind, dressed as an admiralty judge. He led a body of dignitaries, at whose head "ten gentlemen marched . . . arm in arm," signifying the ten ratifying states (Hazard 1828, 418).[6] This body of worthies served to illustrate the current state of the national union coalescing under the Constitution and to introduce the twin themes of the celebration: the construction, both figurative and literal, of the new nation from its own materials and the opportunities available to all Americans as contributors to and, tacitly, beneficiaries of its completion.

The first of these, the float for the Carpenters' Company, featured a "new roof or grand federal edifice," symbolizing the anticipated national union. It was the first of many prepared and exhibited by Philadelphia's craft and trade associations. Hopkinson himself described the float as "an elegant edifice" whose dome was raised on "thirteen Corinthian columns" with "pedestals proper to that order." Reiterating the unfinished state of the union, ten columns were "complete, with three left unfinished." The dome was rimmed by a "frieze decorated with thirteen stars," and seated within were "representatives of the citizens at large, to whom the constitution was committed." In a cupola topping the dome was a figure of the goddess Plenty with her cornucopia. In all, the float was close to thirty-six feet tall, and its carriage, "drawn by 10 white horses," was inscribed with the motto "IN UNION THE FABRIC STANDS FIRM" (Hazard 1828, 419).

The Carpenters' Company was one of the city's oldest and wealthiest craft brotherhoods, and its members, some 450 architects and master builders, marched under their standard behind the float. They were followed by the saw cutters and file makers with their tools, headed by their masters and carrying a "flag with a hand saw and a saw mill saw," insignia of their trades. The Carpenters were set off from the other craft and trade contingents by a corps of the Society of the Cincinnati, all former continental army or naval officers. They were followed in turn by the Agricultural Society, featuring ploughmen, millers, and a sower tossing seed (ibid.).

Even as the Carpenters' Constitution float passed out of sight, an-

---

[6]Although only nine states had ratified the Constitution at the time of the Grand Federal Procession, the federalists' attention to New York's pending vote may explain the tenth marcher.

other magnificent construction appeared. First came a large blue flag depicting "a beehive standing in the rays of the rising sun," under which marched the investors of the Manufacturing Society, mostly prominent merchants and financiers (Hazard 1828, 419; Davis 1986, 119–20). Behind them came a rolling textile works in miniature, proclaiming the Society's vision of Philadelphia's (and the nation's) future in factory-organized manufactures. Approximately thirty feet long, the float included twelve men and women engaged in the actual production of fabrics. The prominent features, though, were the textile machines—a large carding machine, many-spindled spinning wheels, looms, and a machine for printing "muslins of an elegant chintz pattern"—that the workers tended. Above the workshop stage waved a large Stars and Stripes trimmed with "thirty-seven different . . . specimens of printing done at Philadelphia" (Hazard 1828, 419).

Spectators were immediately treated to a third elaborate display. Led by the Marine Society, "six abreast, with trumpets, spy-glasses, charts," and other emblems of their profession in their hands, the "Federal Ship *Union*" sailed into view (Hazard 1828, 419). The thirty-three-foot ship, its wheels and mechanical works concealed under painted seas (rendered by Charles Wilson Peale), appeared to "sail" along the street. The *Union* "mounting twenty guns," was operated by a captain and a crew of twenty-five, who entertained the crowds by "setting sail, trimming her sails to the wind," and other nautical duties executed "with the strictest maritime propriety." In its wake came naval architects and master shipbuilders and their men, carrying the plans and instruments essential to their occupations. They were followed by "mast makers, caulkers, and workmen, to the amount of 330, all wearing a badge in their hats representing a ship on the stocks and a green sprig of white oak." Within this contingent another maritime float represented a shipbuilder's shop, inside which a longboat "was nearly completed during the procession." Those port trades that didn't mount floats marched as groups—rope makers, chandlers, joiners—and displayed emblems or tools of their specialties; many carried banners and flags. In most cases masters led, followed by their journeymen and apprentices. A second band of musicians punctuated the display of the city's major commercial powers' great floats (Hazard 1828, 419–20; Silverman 1987, 583–84).

Philadelphia's diverse individual artisans, representing over forty distinct trades, came next. Although they were independent producers, they marched under the banners of their respective guilds—coach painters, porters, gilders, blacksmiths, hatters, glovers, stone cutters, barbers, tobacconists, instrument makers, clock makers, cabinetmakers, brick makers, printers, stationers, and bookbinders, among others. Many constructed small floats on which they displayed their skills or from which they distributed samples to the crowds. Printers, on a float with a working press, struck off and handed out copies of a "Federal Ode" that Hopkinson had composed. Coppersmiths repaired old kettles, and blacksmiths formed sickles from rusty old swords. Interspersed between the numerous groups of different craftsmen were units of "light cavalry, infantry and militia" (Hazard 1828, 420–21; Bell 1962, 12).

At the end of the train of artisans came representatives of government—members of Congress, state legislators, and city council and other civic officials—with lawyers, physicians, and "the clergy of the different Christian denominations, with the rabbi of the Jews, walking arm in arm." Yet another band accompanied them. Finally, under a banner that read "The rising generation" came an assembly of students from the University of Pennsylvania and other city schools led by their professors, masters, and tutors. Closing the procession, and echoing the cavalry escort at its head, rode a county troop of horse (Hazard 1828, 423).

On reaching Union Green, marchers and spectators were banqueted and entertained with toasts and speeches. The "Grand Federal Edifice" and "Federal Ship *Union*" floats were brought to rest inside a five-hundred-foot circle of tables, which was lined with casks of porter, "Federal beer and cyder." Nearly half the city's population, an estimated seventeen thousand persons, joyously joined in the toasts offered from the domed platform of the "Federal Edifice." Ten toasts, the first to "The people of the United States" and the last to "The whole family of mankind," were drunk, each announced by trumpets and answered by the *Rising Sun*'s cannon. The afternoon concluded with speeches from the rolling rostrum (Hazard 1828, 423; *New York Packet*).

The decision to mount the Philadelphia celebration on 4 July was deliberate and strategic. Earlier, local celebrations had usually taken place within a few days of each state's ratification: Boston's came two days after Massachusetts' approval; Baltimore's followed Maryland's ratification by four days; similar timing can also be seen in the examples of New Haven, Connecticut; Trenton, New Jersey; and Charleston, South Carolina. Philadelphia's Grand Federal Procession, on the other hand, was delayed almost three weeks (Silverman 1987, 581–82).

The obvious reason for such a delay, of course, was to take advantage of the anniversary of the Declaration of Independence. By holding their celebration on Independence Day, federalist organizers were able to capitalize on, and even exploit, the occasion and the sentiments it engendered (Maier 1977, 170). The city was accustomed to large crowds assembling for its annual ceremonial festivities, reports of which were generally well circulated in the other states' major presses. The presence of a large audience for the Grand Federal Procession, as well as vendors of food and drink, ready accommodations, and attentive journalists, was thus virtually guaranteed (Davis 1986, 40–45, 63–69, 132). The Philadelphia federalists also had a less obvious reason for delaying their celebration, however. Although New Hampshire's ratification assured the adoption of the Constitution, New York legislators had not yet embraced it. As one of the largest states, New York's voluntary acceptance of the new federal system was considered essential to its success. The state's leaders, and to a lesser extent its citizens, had lately been the objects of an ambitious campaign of persuasion in the state's newspapers. When New York's ratifying convention met in Poughkeepsie that May, however, the delegates had opposed the Constitution two to one; the popular vote was 56 percent against (Wills 1982, xii–xiii; Howard 1989, 3–18, 130–36; Wiebe 1984, 31–40, 87). Knowing that detailed accounts of their activities would be recounted in New York papers, the Philadelphia federalists no doubt kept an anxious eye on the reaction in Poughkeepsie.

New York's eventual acceptance of the federal system and the Constitution certainly cannot be attributed solely to the celebration in Philadelphia or even to the one in New York City, which was characterized by many parallels with the Philadelphia event. Such causality was more than a theoretical possibility for the federalists, however. In the republican ideology that guided the federalist impulse, the government *was* the people; they were the source of its authority, power, and legitimacy. Such an understanding, perforce, conflates the separate tasks put forth in Rush's "Address to the People"; regardless of legislative approval, the federalists' "new forms of government" can only be "brought to perfection" when the people whom it embodies are prepared in "principles, morals and manners." If their project was to be sustained, the federalists recognized a need for the same network of harmonious social relations and personal affiliations that had supported the old corporate ideal. In short, the federalist enterprise was culture building as well as nation building.

Whether Dr. Rush anticipated the Grand Federal Procession in his January 1787 "Address to the People" is an intriguing question, especially in light of the events that followed. Although he was deeply involved with the push toward constitutional federalism, and clearly played a prominent role in Philadelphia's celebration, there is no clear link or direct causal connection to support that degree of premeditation. To assure the project's success, on the other hand, Rush seems to have recognized the need to establish a cultural foundation for the new

Constitution that was as strong as the legislative one. His address implied that like the earlier resistance to Parliament's punitive acts, the movement toward independence, and the prosecution of the war, this new government would only prosper to the extent that it agreed with the "principles, morals and manners" of the people (Maier 1977, 7–16, 59–68; Shaw 1981, 5–8, 229–31; Howard 1989, 82).

Rush also recognized that he and his fellow federalists would have to "prepare" the populace for such agreement. Acceptance of the idea of federalism had been far from unanimous; the debates of the Constitutional Convention had been contentious and had frequently stalled until the delegates crafted a compromise. As the document went to the states for ratification, the votes of the more recalcitrant became the most important. The federalists staged the processions in the major cities of the various states as each ratified the Constitution. As the number of ratifying states grew, the festivities also took on a propagandistic function, urging those remaining to complete the job. Local papers circulated reports of each event widely. These reports, along with editorial arguments like those of Hamilton's, Jay's, and Madison's *Federalist* articles, served to create a sense of momentum, if not inevitability, to the Constitution's ultimate adoption. Thus, despite its festive air, its broad participation, the Federal Procession was a decidedly political performance (Young 1984, 200; Main 1961, 9, 10).

The efficacy of the Federal Processions is a somewhat more open question. For most of its history federal discourse has only infrequently been challenged. As public performances, though, the answer is easier to see. With its marchers massed under colorful banners and flags, animated floats and pageants, music and spectacle, the Grand Federal Procession was undeniably a memorable event. As Anna Clifford, a Quaker visitor to Philadelphia and witness to the procession, wrote in a letter to her sister, the question of the new government's success aside, "the pageantry of the day will not soon be forgotten, it was altogether a most magnificent shew, superior several English gentlemen said to any thing of the kind they ever saw in Europe" (Clifford 1788, 280).

Works Cited

Albanese, Catherine L. 1976. *Sons of the Fathers: The Civil Religion of the American Revolution*. Philadelphia: Temple University Press.

Beer, Samuel H. 1993. *To Make a Nation: The Rediscovery of American Federalism*. Cambridge: Harvard University Press.

Bell, Whitfield J., Jr. 1962. "The Federal Procession of 1788." *New York Historical Society Quarterly Bulletin* 46 (January): 5–39.

Butterfield, Lyman H., ed. 1951. *Letters of Benjamin Rush*. Princeton: Princeton University Press.

Clifford, Anna. 1788. Letter to Sarah Dowell Clifford, 11 July. Pemberton Papers, Clifford Correspondence, VIII, 278–80. Historical Society of Pennsylvania.

Davis, Susan G. 1986. *Parades and Power*. Philadelphia: Temple University Press.

Fearnow, Mark. 1992. "American Colonial Disturbances as Political Theatre." *Theatre Survey* 33 (May): 53–64.

Fischer, David Hackett. 1989. *Albion's Seed: Four British Folkways in America*. New York: Oxford University Press.

Gilje, Paul A. 1987. *The Road to Mobocracy: Popular Disorder in New York City, 1763–1834*. Chapel Hill: Published for the Institute of Early American History and Culture by the University of North Carolina Press.

Hazard, Samuel, ed. 1828. *Register of Pennsylvania* (Philadelphia).

Hopkinson, Francis. [1788] 1828. "An Account of the Federal Procession of July 4, 1788." Originally published in *American Museum* 4 July. Reprinted in Samuel Hazard, *Register of Pennsylvania*, pp. 417–25.

Howard, Dick. 1989. *The Birth of American Political Thought*. Minneapolis: University of Minnesota Press.

Kammen, Michael. 1987. *A Machine That Would Go of Itself: The Constitution in American Culture*. New York: Vintage.

Kramnick, Isaac, and Michael Foot, eds. 1987. *Thomas Paine Reader*. London: Penguin.

Lafayette, Marquis de. 1781. Letter to the Compte de Maurepas, 20 October. In *Lafayette in the Age of the American Revolution: Selected Letters and Papers*, ed. Stanley J. Idzerda et al. Vol. 4. Ithaca: Cornell University Press.

Maier, Pauline. 1977. *American Scripture: Making the Declaration of Independence*. New York: Knopf.

Main, Jackson T. 1961. *The Anti-Federalists: Critics of the Constitution, 1781–1788*. Chapel Hill: University of North Carolina Press.

New York Packet. 1788. 22 July. n.p.

Richards, Jeffrey. 1991. *Theater Enough: American Culture and the Metaphor of the World Stage, 1607–1789*. Durham, N.C.: Duke University Press.

Rigal, Laura. 1996. "'Raising the Roof': Authors, Spectators, and Artisans in the Grand Federal Procession of 1788." *Theatre Journal* 48 (October): 253–78.

Rush, Benjamin. 1787. "An Address to the People of the United States." *American Museum*, 7 January.

———. 1788. "Observations on the Grand Federal Procession by a Gentleman in This City." *American Museum, or Repository of Ancient and Modern Fugitive Pieces* (c. July): 75–79.

Shaw, Peter. 1981. *American Patriots and the Rituals of Revolution*. Cambridge, Mass.: Harvard University Press.

Silverman, Kenneth. 1987. *A Cultural History of the American Revolution*. New York: Columbia University Press.

Solberg, Winton. 1977. *Redeem the Time: The Puritan Sabbath in Early America.* Cambridge: Harvard University Press.

Wiebe, Robert H. 1984. *Opening of American Society: From the Adoption of the Constitution to the Eve of Disunion.* New York: Knopf.

Wilentz, Sean. 1983. "Artisan Republican Festivals and the Rise of Class Conflict in New York City, 1788–1837." In *Working-Class America: Essays in Labor, Community, and American Society,* ed. Michael Frich and Daniel Walkowitz, pp. 37–77. Urbana: University of Illinois Press.

———. 1984. *Chants Democratic: New York City and the Rise of the American Working Class, 1788–1850.* New York: Oxford University Press.

Wills, Garry, ed. 1982. Introduction to *The Federalist Papers by Alexander Hamilton, James Madison, and John Jay.* New York: Bantam.

Young, Alfred F. 1984. "English Plebeian Culture and Eighteenth-Century American Radicalism." In *The Origin of Anglo-American Radicalism,* ed. Margaret Jacob and James Jacob. London: Allen and Unwin.

The Perpetual Present

Life as Art during the 1960s

David Callaghan

I N THE RECENTLY AIRED two-part television series *The '60s,* the characters of the Herlihy siblings—working-class kids from Chicago who become radicalized and "turn on, tune in, and drop out" in various ways—find themselves seemingly participating in every iconic, socially significant event of the era. For instance, they are all reunited at Woodstock (no doubt the odds for being struck by lightning would have been better) and then rush home for a huggy reconciliation with their conservative "establishment" father. Before dropping acid at Woodstock, however, teenage runaway Katie Herlihy flees the poverty of street life in San Francisco's Haight-Ashbury to join a friend on the Hog Farm commune in New Mexico. Their community is represented as a countercultural paradise, where its members have nothing better to do than sit around and philosophize while Katie looks agog at the huge bowls of fresh vegetables cluttering the set. Naturally, she only spends enough time there for the viewer to see "Wavy Gravy"—one of the Hog Farm's founders and perhaps best-known personality—utter his often-quoted line about providing security at Woodstock with "seltzer bottles and cream pies."

This visual and aural dash through the 1960s offers a facile and sanitized version of that era in the service of "February Sweeps." (That discussion, however, is another paper.) The brief glimpse of the Hog Farm, for example, equally distorts and cheapens the hard work and courage of this group and others that attempted to blur the boundaries between art and life during the 1960s and beyond.

Interest in this topic (the relationship between life and art), of course, predates the 1960s. Russian playwright and theorist Nikolas Evreinoff

engaged the subject in the 1920s with his collection of essays *The Theatre in Life*. Evreinoff claims that the instinct to "play" is fundamental
to human nature and that we constantly play parts in the everyday activities of society. Marvin Carlson notes that Evreinoff's major points
were echoed in later "role and performance" theory, as with the better-
known and frequently cited writings of Kenneth Burke and Erving
Goffman in the 1940s and 1950s (Carlson 1996, 34–39). In the late 1960s
and early 1970s, however, critics like Richard Schechner, Elizabeth
Burns, and Bruce Wilshire participated in an ongoing debate about the
essential nature of "role playing" or "performance" in life. In her book
Theatricality Burns contended that because a constant "feed in and
feed-back" between the stage and life exists, theatre tends to formalize,
if not idealize, the rituals that permeate all aspects of our daily life
(quoted in Carlson 1984, 482–83). Schechner, who wrote about performance theory in the *Drama Review* during the 1960s and later in
such books as *Ritual, Play, and Performance* and *Essays on Performance
Theory,* strongly emphasized the difference between theatre and ritual,
asserting that "theatre" offered entertainment for a passive, separate
audience, whereas ritual merged the two in various participatory acts
(1977, 60–62; Carlson 1984, 483–84). Finally, Bruce Wilshire adopted a
different stance in his book *Role Playing and Identity: The Limits of
Theatre as Metaphor.* Wilshire argued against "aestheticizing" the notion
of social roles because they contain inherently spontaneous, and ethical,
impulses that work outside the realm of repeatable action or drama.
Thus, he envisioned more of a boundary between on- and offstage behavior than do Burns or Evreinoff (Wilshire 1982, 280–81; Carlson 1996,
44–45).

   This dialogue indicates that the aesthetic and philosophical notion of
"life as art" has been the source of a spirited, ongoing controversy involving a number of artists and critics and has continued and intensified
as the lines between conventional theatre and "performance" have become increasingly blurred in recent years. Thus, the groups considered
in this essay were hardly alone in their consideration of this premise,
but they did attempt to implement their ideas in ways singularly unique
and influential. What follows, then, will examine how certain collectives
or loosely interconnected tribes of social activists and artists adopted
an aesthetic and social paradigm that perceived day-to-day life as a performance of sorts. In doing so they helped to redefine and stretch the
boundaries of what could be construed as acting and theatre and seized
on the possibilities of art and performance as a means of creating a new
social order in America.

   Although the Hog Farm (as well as Ken Kesey's Merry Pranksters) achieved a degree of national notoriety even during the 1960s, there were hundreds of lesser-known collectives in this period that were pursuing similar agendas. Many of these surrogate families did not survive the period, although offshoots of or groups resembling the Hog Farm and the Free Family still thrive today. Interestingly, the origins of the three social collectives that are the focus of my discussion—the Diggers, the Free Family, and the Hog Farm—are to be found in the growing dissatisfaction with the Stanislavski-influenced training and "realistic" conventions that dominated American theatre at the beginning of the 1960s. For example, Wavy Gravy—then known as Hugh Romney— studied with Sanford Meisner at the Neighborhood Playhouse in New York City before abandoning the conventional theatre to pursue a guerrilla form of stand-up comedy that eventually led him to the theatrical underground movements of the West Coast (Gravy 1992, 227–29). Similarly, Peter Coyote, today a well-known film actor, began his career with the West Coast Actor's Workshop before discovering the more radical, politically motivated San Francisco Mime Troupe in the same neighborhood. In his recent memoir, *Sleeping Where I Fall*, Coyote notes that he was attracted to the Mime Troupe's aesthetic and political objective of removing theatre from the socially encoded confines of formally defined stages and placing it in the public streets and parks of America. In doing so the troupe and other companies like it effectively removed the signifiers or "rules"—such as clearly defined roles for spectators, performers, stage, and audience (what Michael Kirby once referred to as theatre's "information structure")—that had previously defined the conventional theatre-going experience (Kirby 1965, 28). Without these signifiers to generate meaning, viewers could no longer passively observe a theatrical event and, in the aesthetic of these radicals, "hide" behind such barriers. Instead, they would be forced to acknowledge the conventions of performance, to decipher its codes, since they were often presented as an element of daily public activity and typically drew nearby life events (e.g., traffic noise) into the "play." Thus, in theory each audience member would potentially be able to engage the work on his or her own personalized terms (Coyote 1998, 7–15, 32–38).

Work of this sort, although redefining the "rules of the game," still operated within the context of what Kirby calls "matrixed" performing (Kirby 1965, 26). Coyote and his fellow Mime Troupe members were playing fictional roles for an audience, which would eventually acknowledge the event as a performance with their applause and, hopefully, a donation, at which point all would return home to their other, separate, "real" lives. Kirby speaks to a more radical extension of such work in his discussion of nonmatrixed events or "happenings," in which the "performer" ceases to play a character. As Kirby himself puts it, "he attempts to be no one other than himself, nor does he function in a place other than that which physically contains him and the audience" (1965, 25–26).

Similarly, Viola Spolin's influential work in the area of improvisation also influenced theatrical efforts to break down barriers and limitations during this period. In her words: "We cannot approach . . . intuition until we are free of opinions, attitude, judgments, prejudices; and the very act of seeking the moment, of being open to fellow players, produces a life force, a flow, a regeneration, for all who participate" (Spolin, interviewed in Law 1991).

Kirby's notion of "non-acting" was embodied in the work of influential theatre collectives of the period such as the Living Theatre, Open Theatre, and the Performance Group, which privileged the presence of the actor over traditional conceptions of character and role in various high-profile avant-garde productions throughout the 1960s. Another strand of artists, however, such as Coyote, Wavy Gravy, and their peers sought to go even further in their quest to live "in the art" and thus increasingly blur the perceptual boundaries between art and life. Mime Troupe member Peter Berg used the term *life-actor* to describe the kind of artist who could abandon socially imposed restrictions in order to create his or her own life-role on a daily basis (Coyote 1998, 20, 33–35). Such impulses led Berg, Coyote, and a number of like-minded individuals to join a locally based activist group known as the Diggers, who contended that all theatrical performance, as well as the counterculture itself, had been co-opted by the capitalist consumer system as a means of making profit. For them, the alternative was to create life performance events for free that would not support the larger establishment systems. The Diggers encouraged each individual to imagine his or her ideal society and to strive to create it regardless of personal, social, or economic consequences (Coyote 1998, 63–66). Each life-actor would construct a persona that embodied this ideal and then perform it in his or her daily existence. As Coyote put it, "in this way, each of us might become his or her own hero, as well as an engine of social change" (1998, 65).

The Diggers soon created a series of freewheeling activities around San Francisco to explore these parameters. Some of the more colorful ones included burning ten-dollar bills in public; operating a "free" store where the "managers" encouraged the "customers" to "steal" the goods; and dispensing food to area street people, who were then asked to step through an oversized "free frame of perception" (Coyote 1998, 80–91; see also Grogan 1990, 233–412; Law 1991; Taylor 1987, 192–93).

In all instances perceptions about the roles of "employees" or "consumers" within the larger socioeconomic order was challenged by the Diggers' life-actors. This dynamic was creatively demonstrated by Ron Thelin (co-owner of the Haight's Psychedelic Shop and later a member of one of the Free Family's collective outposts), who set up and ate a full-course dinner—complete with linen tablecloths and crystal—along the freeway. As Coyote observed about the event, "[T]he suggestion was that if you wanted to get out of your car and eat—what was stopping you?" (Taylor 1987, 201).

After the so-called summer of love in 1967, many of the Diggers abandoned the city and created a web of loosely connected, rurally based communities that became known as the Free Family. The Hog Farm experienced a similar evolutionary process, which began when a group of the Merry Pranksters were left stranded at Wavy Gravy's place in Los Angeles in 1965. Soon afterward, the group accepted an invitation to live for free on a hog farm outside the city in exchange for tending the hogs (Coyote 1998, 131–58; Gravy 1992, 12–23). The formation of these communities represents the final evolution of the nonmatrixed performance aesthetic created by the 1960s avant-garde. These social collectives were no longer interested in staging performances within any kind of structured framework but sought rather to embody the notion of art, acting, and performance through daily communal living.

It is important to point out that their efforts to live in the "perpetual present" were not motivated by self-indulgence, although they were driven by a high level of idealism and perhaps naiveté. Certainly some collectives of the period sought isolation from those aspects of American society that they disliked, and the communal movements, in general, inevitably attracted individual slackers and hustlers who were looking for a free ride. But the core members of these groups, by committing to personal authenticity and acting out their inner dreams and directives, were seeking to create an alternative culture that could offer its members and their fellow citizens more creatively rewarding and enlightened possibilities in life. As Coyote recalls, "[O]ur hope was that if we were imaginative enough in creating paradigms as free men and women, the example would be infectious and might produce self-directed (as opposed to coerced or manipulated) social change. If this were to occur en masse, it would engender significant changes in our society" (1998, 70).

In addition to setting up communal bases, these groups caravaned across America in order to maximize their impact on the larger culture. According to Wavy Gravy, this mission began with "hog Sunday" celebrations that materialized when friends showed up to spend the day engaging in activities that centered on themes such as "dress like kids" and "roll in the mud" or participating in events like the "hog rodeo." Like some currents of the Free Family, the group eventually piled into buses and trucks and went on the road for extended periods of time beginning in 1967 (Law 1991; see also Gravy 1992, 229–30). In the case of the Hog Farm, they presented mixed-media events around the country, which former Hog Farmer David Lebrun describes:

> Wavy Gravy discovered in work with autistic children that he could get children who wouldn't talk to or touch each other to talk and make contact using improvisational methods. Operating on the assumption that by the late sixties the whole world was very autistic, very polarized, out of touch but actually wanting to make contact, we used these techniques and went right into middle America. The Hog Farm happenings were aimed at an entire community—church, police, students—people who didn't usually talk to each other. . . . Camp would be like a circus. . . . [T]he police would always stop us, but we learned to switch roles, so, rather than them just being police and us being hippies, we would change all the parts around. We would start taking movies of them, asking them to take pictures of us playing "Home on the Range" to them on kazoos, or getting out all kinds of toys, and the police would be disarmed. . . . It was very powerful. (quoted in Taylor 1987, 99–100)

Indeed, several influential sociologists, theorists, and psychologists of this period, such as Charles Reich and R. D. Laing, contributed to and documented this link between a new consciousness and concrete social change in the 1960s. Perhaps none did so quite as succinctly as Reich in his book *The Greening of America*. Reich speaks of the vision of those who sought life in the "perpetual present" in his discussion of the need for young people to "recover the self" in the 1960s. Reich believed that once this higher state of consciousness was achieved, each individual must assume responsibility for those "who seem to be enemies but are only the deceived, the broken, the lost" (1971, 321). Indeed, the closing passage of his book aptly captures the nonviolent, revolutionary idealism of the Free Family and the Hog Farm: "We have all been induced to give up our dreams of adventure and romance in favor of . . . success, but . . . the dream is real. And these things, buried, hidden, and disowned in so many of us, are shouted out loud, believed in, affirmed by a growing multitude of young people who seem too healthy, intelligent, and alive to be wholly insane, who appear, in their collective strength, to be making it happen" (1971, 429–30).

One of the key principles of this desired new social order was the notion of living in present time without any immediate preconceived agendas or goals (hence the impulse of the above-mentioned groups to take to the road). Coyote's memoir reflects this way of thinking when, for instance, he discusses how his "family" kept their trucks going by constantly salvaging and repairing discarded parts. He and his peers would often spend days on such activities because they had the time to do so (Coyote 1998, 130–33). Although on one level this could be perceived as shiftless behavior, Coyote observed that "the investiture of time conferred value. . . . [W]ho but a free person had the time to wire brush and lovingly retrofit each old part necessary to the reassembly of a vehicle? We were happy to live with society's garbage because we had the time to recycle and reclaim it" (1998, 133). Indeed, "getting off the bus" of consumer capitalism through the pursuit of such mundane activities resonated with revolutionary implications and reflected the evolutionary journey of these former "actors" who now sought to "perform" in the "present-time" by constructing their daily routines or doing freely chosen work. As Richard Albert, later known as Ram Dass, observed about the 1960s some twenty years later, "the minute we saw there was relative reality, we were empowered to change things" (interviewed in Law 1991). In the purely aesthetic realm, Viola Spolin echoed and supported the ideology of the "free" tribes of the era:

> Do not consider present time as clock time. But rather as a timeless moment when all are mutually engaged and experiencing an outcome of which is yet unknown. See—you're right there—you're connected and you don't know what's gonna happen and that's where the excitement is and that's where the spontaneity is and that's where the vitality is and that's where the joy is and that's where the happiness is and that's the everlasting, never-ending spiral. (interviewed in Law 1991)

But what of the spiral of the 1960s and the work of the various groups under consideration? Although much of the social fervor and experimentation of the period waned by the mid-1970s, the distinctive aesthetic and social activism of the Hog Farmers, Diggers, Free Family, and others like them represents an important populist strand of the politically oriented avant-garde current of the 1960s. Unlike groups like the Weathermen who advocated violence as a means to achieve revolution, these collectives used their artistic imaginations and daily labor to create free-spirited, authentically committed lives that served as a model for possible change in the larger culture. And although radical, politically activist theatre companies like the Living Theatre also lived communally in order to merge art and life, they nonetheless operated within the boundaries of performance spaces, albeit nontraditional ones in many instances. In contrast, the groups under consideration sought to explore the intersection between the aesthetic, personal, and political realms of existence beyond the context of any formal theatrical or performative frames. As artist T. A. Price noted about the Hog Farm, "[Y]ou had to be a good actor in this movie which is our lives" (interviewed in Law 1991).

Still, key life-actors in these movements, such as Coyote and Wavy Gravy, have openly acknowledged and engaged the excesses, drug casualties, and mistakes of the 1960s and their own lofty—and at times equally irresponsible—lifestyle and ideology. As Coyote wryly observed in *Sleeping Where I Fall*, how could such "self-appointed heroes" be bothered with the ongoing burdens of cleaning dishes or scrubbing toilets? (1998, 291). Consequently, many of these collectives fell short of their goals and collapsed because of internal strife or their members' unwillingness to accept responsibility for the maintenance of their communities. Nonetheless, although they have weathered a constantly shifting membership over the years, both the Hog Farm and components of the Free Family still exist and continue to evolve. The Hog Farm is now located on a ranch north of San Francisco, where it supports various small businesses, as well as a myriad of socially engaged causes. In addition, it runs Camp Winnarainbow for teenagers, which allows members to pass on the life-actor techniques from the 1960s to new generations of young people. Similarly, Free Family outposts like the Black Bear Ranch in California are still functioning, and members like Coyote and Peter Berg continue to advocate many of the same ideological principles in the 1990s (see Coyote 1998, 157–58, 349–51; Gravy 1992, 22–26, 146–55; Law 1991; Sheppard 1987).

Their legacy is complex and ongoing, but these artists certainly represent a little-known but uniquely colorful chapter in the history of "theatre at the margins." Although their greatest contribution lies perhaps in their long-term efforts to make the planet a better place for future generations, they forged a provocative and influential means of effecting that change during the 1960s. In doing so they greatly contributed to the expansion of previously held notions of theatre and performance that occurred in this era and thus prefigured post-1960s avant-garde developments in "performance art" and the impulse to meld life and art in the "perpetual present."[1]

---

[1]Although I have tried to place their aesthetic and political ideology in the context of other marginal avant-garde groups of the era, my main emphasis has been to evaluate, and acknowledge, their singular contribution to the dynamic zeitgeist of the 1960s.

Works Cited

Burns, Elizabeth. 1972. *Theatricality*. London: Longman.

Carlson, Marvin. 1984. *Theories of the Theatre*. Ithaca: Cornell University Press.

———. 1996. *Performance*. New York: Routledge.

Coyote, Peter. 1998. *Sleeping Where I Fall*. Washington, D.C.: Counterpoint Press.

Evreinoff, Nikolas. 1927. *The Theatre in Life*. Trans. Alexander Nazaroff. New York: Brentano's.

Gravy, Wavy (Hugh Romney). 1992. *Something Good for a Change*. New York: St. Martin's.

Grogan, Emmett. 1990. *Ringolevio*. New York: Citadel Press.

Kirby, Michael. 1965. "The New Theatre." *Drama Review* 10 (winter): 23–43.

Law, Lisa, dir. 1991. *Flashing on the Sixties*. Videocassette. Pyramid Film and Video.

Reich, Charles A. 1971. *The Greening of America*. New York: Bantam.

Schechner, Richard. 1977. *Essays on Performance Theory 1970–76*. New York: Drama Book Specialists.

Sheppard, John, dir. 1987. *It Was Twenty Years Ago Today*. Granada Television.

Taylor, Derek. 1987. *It Was Twenty Years Ago Today*. New York: Simon and Schuster.

The '60s. 1999. NBC Television. 7 and 8 February.

Wilshire, Bruce. 1982. *Role Playing and Identity: The Limits of Theatre as Metaphor*. Bloomington: Indiana University Press.

Teetering at the Margins

The Evolution of *Hair,* the American Tribal Love-Rock Musical

Martha S. LoMonaco

*H*AIR, the "American tribal love-rock musical" that evolved rapidly from a low-budget pacan to antiestablishment values and the hippie lifestyle to a big-budget commercial phenomenon, provides a fascinating glimpse into the contradictory politics and philosophies that characterized both American society and its theatre during the 1960s. In October 1967 producer Joseph Papp opened *Hair* as the premiere production of the Anspacher/Public Theatre, the new home of the heavily subsidized New York Shakespeare Festival in the heart of the downtown Manhattan art scene. By April 1968 producer Michael Butler, who had purchased the exclusive rights from Papp, opened a reconceived *Hair* at the uptown Biltmore Theatre. Butler's production went on to become one of the longest-running shows in Broadway history.

Once the musical had proven to be a commercial hit, Butler fabricated an empire that spawned new productions of *Hair* in major cities and sent touring companies to smaller towns throughout the United States and abroad. By 1977 the show had grossed $80 million, had played throughout the world, and was reaping additional profits from eleven original cast albums. It also inspired over sixty cover versions of celebrated show tunes that became number one hits on the pop music charts. Seemingly without irony Butler proclaimed the show, which made him a very rich man, "a demonstrative rejection of materialism." Yet the *Hair* empire spun a web of tangled finances, legal issues, and disgruntled employees, all of which are the antithesis of the show's message. How could a play extolling a simple life filled with peace, love, and happiness turn into a multimillion-dollar business? How did *Hair* transform from its countercultural beginnings in lower Manhattan into an international, mainstream commodity, and why?

Hair was the brainchild of two actors, James Rado and Gerome Ragni, who wanted to create a theatre experience that mirrored the concerns and ideals of their generation. Both had respectable careers on and off Broadway and, in the case of Ragni, in experimental environments such as the Open Theatre and La Mama E. T. C. Yet they realized that none of the theatre pieces in which they performed had the vibrancy and inherent theatricality of Greenwich Village street culture and Central Park "Be-Ins," which were filled with long-haired youth sporting colorful, often outrageous, "costumes" and wildly painted faces, loud rock-and-roll music, and the tantalizing odors of incense and marijuana. They admired not only the audacious theatricality of youth culture but also its underlying ideology, shaped by a wholesale rejection of establishment values as promulgated by authority figures ranging from parents and teachers to police and the federal government. Important influences included "New Left" political groups such as Students for a Democratic Society (SDS), which advocated a radical transformation (if not abolition) of the military-industrial complex; the civil rights movement, which championed the right of black Americans to be free and equal citizens under the law; and the antiwar movement, which grew in size and urgency with the increasing escalation of the Vietnam War.

Taking their cue from this spirit of protest and rebellion, and sympathizing with the causes that fomented dissent, the authors decided to mount a like-minded assault against their own "establishment"—the Broadway theatre. By bringing both the youth culture and its concerns to the Broadway stage they could, in effect, turn Broadway upside down while simultaneously gaining a powerful platform from which to air their perspectives. What they perhaps failed to consider, however, was how a show celebrating marginality in both form and content could maintain its integrity within a commercial milieu that celebrated little more than box office receipts. Could marginal theatre become commercially successful and still remain marginal?

It is clear from the earliest versions of the script, now available in the Joseph Papp/New York Shakespeare Festival Archives at the New York Public Library for the Performing Arts, that Rado and Ragni, regardless of any consequences, were intent on producing *Hair* on Broadway. The five pages of single-spaced explanatory notes preceding the dialogue describe the transformation of a Broadway-style proscenium theatre into an open environment suitable for their production. They also wrote the script and lyrics (the score was yet to come) in the style of a conven-

tional book musical. Structurally, *Hair* was a dialogue-heavy script interspersed with songs that featured three leads, seven secondary characters, and a large chorus. The story—also fairly conventional—concerned a love triangle (Sheila, Berger, and Claude) and the conflicting
relations as one of them wrestles with the dilemma of whether to serve
in Vietnam. Decidedly unconventional, however, were the characters—
sixteen-to-twenty-year-olds who exemplified the hippie lifestyle; the language—hip colloquialisms and four-letter words; onstage action—characters having sex, smoking pot, and desecrating American icons such as
the flag, the Catholic Church, and Jesus Christ; the proposed staging—
an unmasked, stripped-down theatre with dirt floor; and performers
transforming in and out of character onstage in front of the audience
(Ragni and Rado 1966).

To further explain their concept and rationale, the authors offered
detailed production notes, citing media guru Marshall McLuhan as a
major influence:

> Marshall McLuhan describes today's world as a "global village." And to-
> day's youth is involved in group-tribal activity. So HAIR should be a
> group-tribal activity. An extension of what's happening. A coming-to-
> gether for a common reason: a search for a way of life that makes sense
> to the young, that allows the growth of their new vision, however defined
> or undefined that may be; to find an alternative to the accepted standards,
> goals and morals of the older generation, the establishment. It's what's
> happening now. (Ragni and Rado 1966)

"THE KIDS," as Ragni and Rado described the company, "are a tribe."
The actors were to present themselves simultaneously as characters in a
play, as storytellers demonstrating their way of life, and as performers
acknowledging the theatrical environment. The purpose was to per-
suade the audience of their good intentions in the hopes of gaining
understanding, support, and tolerance for their vision of a "better, saner,
peace-full, love-full world" (Ragni and Rado 1966). The musical was
essentially an exercise in Brecht's alienation effect with love beads, flow-
ers, and a marijuana haze.

It was the "freshness and honesty" of this vision that attracted Joseph
Papp when he received this early version of *Hair* from theatrical agent
Janet Roberts in the fall of 1966. In a letter rejecting her proposal of
Robert Lowell's adaptation of *The Oresteia* as offering "nothing new,"
Papp extolled Ragni and Rado for having "much more to say [than
Lowell] about the human condition. . . . The work at present is sprawl-
ing, which is part of its power, but we all agree that it needs considerable
work," he contended, pledging that the Shakespeare Festival was willing

to work with the playwrights in a manner that would be "sensitive to their style" (Papp 1966). It was presumably much the same script that attracted composer Galt MacDermot, who was looking to score music for an offbeat show. MacDermot was attracted to the idea of a rock-and-roll musical in which he could mix rock, jazz, and African rhythms. He told an interviewer that "he took the lyrics home" and "could hear melodies to those words," and composed the score in four days (Sandrow 1977).

Although Papp did not offer a Broadway venue, he was a powerful and respected New York producer who was giving the show a chance to be seen. Papp formally optioned *Hair* in March 1967 and named as the show's director Shakespeare Festival Artistic Director Gerald Freedman, who had been working with Ragni and Rado in developing the script. They lured the politically charged choreographer Anna Sokolow, known as the inventor of social protest ballets, to join the production team. In a letter to Freedman, Sokolow concurred with his assessment of the show as fresh, audacious, and "really naive at times" and agreed that the production demanded "a true sense of innocence and honesty, and no phony effects language wise and otherwise. . . . But the true statement," she proclaimed, "and there *is one*, has to be made clear and to the point—so it just isn't one of those 'happening type' shows" (Sokolow 1967a).

As Papp set the production schedule toward an opening on Sunday, 29 October, Freedman continued a prolonged and exasperating period of script revision with the authors, who were resistant to his recommendations. A complicating factor was that Ragni had also been cast as Berger and although Rado desperately wanted to play Claude, Freedman felt he was too old. Once Sokolow came on board, she largely sided with the authors' perspectives, and Freedman found his authority severely undermined. He resigned from the production on 4 October, assuring Papp in a telegram that his decision was in the best interests of both the Public Theatre and the production, which he believed would be a "good show" that "must open on time and in good faith with the public. . . . I think my authority and judgment has been abused to the point where I can no longer effectively work with the authors," he declared, recommending that Sokolow assume full control as director (Freedman 1967a).

Sokolow took over immediately but encountered insurmountable problems of her own in shaping the piece as theatre rather than pure dance. By now *Hair* had become a highly political theatre piece that melded story, song, dance, characters, and a startling array of images in a rich fashion. With only two days until the beginning of previews,

Papp begged Freedman to return; he agreed only on the condition that he be given full control and that Sokolow be fired (Rubin 1973). She was, and she immediately insisted that her name be removed from all mention of the play. In the Papp Archives there are two versions of the original playbill: one with and one without her name (Sokolow 1967b).

The production that opened ten days later was a successful hybrid of Freedman's, Sokolow's, and Ragni, Rado, and MacDermot's work; both critical and audience reaction declared the show a hit. From that point on *Hair* became a vehicle for making money. The first original cast album was recorded on opening day, and Papp was soon in negotiations to move the production to another theatre after the limited eight-week run closed on 10 December. Thus began a series of legal and financial difficulties that would severely diminish the Public Theatre's role in *Hair*'s future, both artistically and fiscally.

In the meantime, however, the show was being touted for its honesty, freshness, and immediacy—everything that the Public's team had hoped to capture in production—as well as its appealing rock-and-roll score. The Anspacher's three-quarter-thrust stage and intimate actor-audience relationship in the 299-seat theatre contributed to the "in-your-face," visceral quality that added to the show's sense of urgency. The onstage rock band was integrated into Ming Cho Lee's platform and scaffolding set; Theoni V. Aldredge's costumes were a fascinating amalgam of jeans, halter tops, and thrift-shop chic; Martin Aronstein's lighting—completely unmasked—was bold, colorful, and startling. The show was raw, cutting-edge, low-cost entertainment. The top ticket price was $2.50 and the top salaries—to the writers and artistic team— were $1000 apiece.

The romance that was the original *Hair* lasted a mere eight weeks. The Public Theatre was a repertory house, and *Hair* had to vacate to make way for *Hamlet*. Papp announced in early November that the production would move to another off-Broadway house, but negotiations weren't completed until mid-December. In the interim Papp had found a potential financier in a Chicago millionaire's son, who had seen the show at the Public and instantaneously had become a true believer. Although a theatrical neophyte and bearing an unimpressive track record of faulty business dealings, Michael Butler finally managed to put together the financing to move *Hair* to a midtown discotheque, the Cheetah, in late December.

In preparation for the move Freedman reentered negotiations with the authors in the hope of affecting major script revisions. He believed the show was fifteen to twenty minutes too long, particularly in the second act, which had been criticized for being a "conventional story told in a conventional manner." Freedman complained to Papp that rather than attacking the major problems of the script, the authors wanted to add another song to a show that already had over twenty pieces of "song material." Other suggested changes would result in a "multiplicity of contradictory images" that would confuse the already complex show even more. "The problem with their material," Freedman lamented, had always been their inability to "simplify and clarify" (Freedman 1967b). For their part the authors complained to Papp, via their attorney, that Freedman refused even to consider their changes, much less implement them. In his exasperated response Papp contended that "if justice were to be served, Mr. Freedman would be awarded the gold medal for patience, tact and integrity, plus a meritorious life-saving medal for preventing artistic suicide of the three authors" (Papp 1967). It was in this embattled state that the Public Theatre entered its final *Hair* collaboration.

Hair at the Cheetah was essentially the Public's production transported rather awkwardly to a venue that was not a theatre nor capable of being transformed into one. A platform stage was erected amid a cavernous dance floor with 687 chairs arranged below it along three sides. Terrible acoustics and a haze caused by patrons' cigarettes made it difficult either to hear or see. The only plus was the discotheque's elaborate lighting, which was used to good effect in the production. Despite the performers' best efforts, the show was undermined by the space, and box office receipts dropped. By late January, Butler, who had incorporated as Natoma Productions, was in dire financial straits; a flurry of legal correspondence and threatened closure notices in the Papp Archive attest to unpaid bills and royalties, union troubles, and general dissatisfaction. The show closed soon after and with it the Public's final artistic connection with *Hair*.

What was undoubtedly a sore point to Papp, and ultimately a major financial loss to the Shakespeare Festival, was that by moving *Hair* to the Cheetah rather than to a "first class situation," he had lost the rights to produce *Hair* in a Broadway house (Schlesinger 1967). Any hopes that Papp and Freedman, who was bitter that he never gained any financial rewards from the show that he had worked so hard to mold, had for reaping the gains of a commercial production were dashed. Although the Shakespeare Festival has always earned royalties from subsequent productions, the amount was minuscule compared to the enormous earnings *Hair* garnered for its new production team.

Michael Butler had higher aspirations from the beginning. Freed from Papp's grasp after the Cheetah disaster, he quickly embarked on a completely reconstituted show under the guidance of Tom O'Horgan, popularly known as "the high priest of off-off-Broadway." He also brought in a totally new artistic team that included scenic designer Robin Wagner, lighting designer Jules Fisher, costume designer Nancy Potts, and choreographer Julie Arnel to implement O'Horgan's concepts. The authors were delighted that they were finally going to see their show not only on Broadway but also as they had always intended it to be (or so they said). What actually happened was that O'Horgan all but eliminated their original book, added even more music (the Broadway version had thirty-three songs), and restructured the piece as a Happening. *Hair* was now a loosely knit musical revue with no discernible plot, one of the first of what later would be termed "concept musicals." The characters were retained but in name only; the substance of their personas and relationships had been cut.

The show's saving grace and the reason it worked for audiences in the late 1960s was that it was firmly entrenched in "the now." O'Horgan could traffic in a theatrical shorthand because the audience filled in the blanks for him. The Vietnam War, *Hair*'s principal thematic link, was screamed out in daily headlines and on the evening news, and by 1968 the antiwar movement was in full swing. Hippies, who were widely assumed to be subsisting on a drug-induced high, weren't expected to make a whole lot of sense, so why should a show celebrating their culture? In addition, the quasi-environmental staging and blurring of performer/audience lines, now an established part of the off-off-Broadway scene, were novel for Broadway audiences. Although the script had all but disappeared, the spirit of the show as originally envisioned by Ragni and Rado was finally being realized, as was the assault on the Broadway establishment. And, happily, audiences seemed thrilled to be a part of it; twenty-four years later one woman waxed rhapsodic in a letter to the editor of the *New York Times* about her memories of Gerome Ragni perched on the arms of her third-row orchestra seat and begging a handout. "I will never forget that, for a minuscule moment," she proclaimed, "I was in the original Broadway production of *Hair*" (Beasley 1993).

The new *Hair* was, to quote critic Charles Marowitz, "riddled with O'Horganisms." Marowitz, who had followed O'Horgan's career in experimental theatre closely, cited "the writhing pantomime; the frantic light effects; the remorseless playing out of physical sub-texts; the bold anti-illusionist devices; and the unabashed gimmickry" as typical of his style (Marowitz 1969). The only distinction, conceded by O'Horgan himself, was his joy at being "more outrageous uptown than I ever was downtown" (Davis 1973, 124). Part of that outrageousness and, some would contend, gimmickry, was the brief nude scene added to the end of act 1. Although Ragni and Rado claimed they had wanted it all along—they had witnessed people joyously stripping at the Central Park "Be-In" that was a major inspiration for the show—there was no nudity during either the Public or Cheetah productions. Although the scene was brief, dimly lit, and optional for performers, it became a major selling point of the show. Witnesses attest to the number of patrons, binoculars in hand, hoping to get a close-up of the first-ever nudity to be seen on Broadway. The entrance of life-like cops "raiding" the theatre moments later, added to the daring and high jinks of the moment.

Voyeurs and sensation-seekers, however, did not constitute the majority of theatregoers, particularly as time went on. Audience surveys attested to the large number of eighteen-to-twenty-five-year-olds—not the usual Broadway crowd—who delighted in seeing performers their own age singing their music and sharing many of their concerns onstage. The show was also a significant draw for middle-class suburbanites, anxious to experience the hippie phenomenon in a safe, controlled environment that nonetheless projected the illusion of an authentic commune.

Ragni and Rado's intended Broadway takeover was thus working, not only onstage, but also at the box office. Ironically, the show celebrated marginality by co-opting the techniques, ideology, and theatregoers normally relegated to the margins as it concurrently celebrated its success as measured in traditional Broadway terms. It is easy to understand the confusion as the lines between the marginal and the mainstream continued to blur with *Hair*'s increasing dominance of both the Broadway stage and major theatres throughout the world. This slippery balance between margins and mainstream actually became the modus operandi for the *Hair* industry as new productions continued to be mounted under the personal supervision of Butler, his staff, and Ragni and Rado, who continued in their dual roles as authors and co-stars. On the one hand, any new production was a carefully controlled replication of the Broadway production; on the other hand, productions were always allowed a good deal of improvisational revision from performance to performance. In this manner *Hair* managed to have its cake and eat it too, which, understandably, was a tantalizing prospect for theatre people who were actually getting paid, and paid well, for reveling in audacious, decidedly unconventional behavior concerning controversial topics.

Although *Hair* encountered more than its share of protest, enforced censorship, and even a U.S. Supreme Court decision that allowed the Boston production to open after being shuttered for eight weeks by the city's district attorney, the show ran successfully throughout the world for a full five years after its premiere. *Hair* became a worldwide commodity because it was the right show, expressing the right sentiments, at the right time, and Butler and company capitalized on the cultural moment. Its simple message extolling the virtues of peace, love, and freedom had universal appeal, particularly in the increasingly complex and troubled times of the late twentieth century. Although people recognized and frequently commented on the commercialism of the show, they generally chose to ignore it in favor of the show's larger virtues. The fact that the producers, in conjunction with a Manhattan retailer named Wig City, were selling an instant male-hippie kit—complete with wigs, beads, bells, and incense—for $29.95 attests to the worst excesses of commodification (unidentified clipping). Yet underneath this rampant commercialism remained a piece of theatre beholden to experimental theatre techniques with a conscience firmly grounded in the precepts of the 1960s counterculture. *Hair* teetered at the margins, co-opting wholesale from both convention and experimentation to create a hybrid unlike any other in Broadway theatre history.

Works Cited

Beasley, Kay. 1993. Letter to the Editor. *New York Times,* 9 May.

Davis, Lorrie. 1973. *Letting Down My Hair: Two Years with the Love Rock Tribe—from Dawning to Downing of Aquarius.* New York: Arthur Fields Books.

Freedman, Gerald. 1967a. Letter to Joseph Papp. 4 October. *T-MSS 1993-028, Box II-79, F7. Joseph Papp/New York Shakespeare Festival Archives. Billy Rose Theatre Collection. New York Public Library for the Performing Arts.

Freedman, Gerald. 1967b. Letter to Joseph Papp. 8 December. *T-MSS 1993-028, Box II-79, F18. Joseph Papp/New York Shakespeare Festival Archives. Billy Rose Theatre Collection. New York Public Library for the Performing Arts.

Marowitz, Charles. 1969. "Existential Thunder." *Village Voice,* 20 February.

Papp, Joseph. 1966. Letter to Janet Roberts, 21 November. *T-MSS 1993-028, Box II-79, F7. Joseph Papp/New York Shakespeare Festival Archives. Billy Rose Theatre Collection. New York Public Library for the Performing Arts.

Papp, Joseph. 1967. Letter to Edward Schlesinger, 28 December. *T-MSS 1993-028, Box II-79, F18. Joseph Papp/New York Shakespeare Festival Archives. Billy Rose Theatre Collection. New York Public Library for the Performing Arts.

Ragni, Gerome, and James Rado. 1966. *Hair, a Musical.* TS *T-MSS 1993-028, Box II-78, F7. Joseph Papp/New York Shakespeare Festival Archives. Billy Rose Theatre Collection. New York Public Library for the Performing Arts.

Rubin, Stephen E. 1973. "Let's 'Hair' It for Gerald Freedman!" *New York Times,* 22 April (clipping). Billy Rose Theatre Collection. *Hair* file. New York Public Library for the Performing Arts.

Sandrow, Nahma. 1977. "What Will 'Hair' Say to the 70's?" *New York Times,* 2 October (clipping). Billy Rose Theatre Collection. *Hair* file. New York Public Library for the Performing Arts.

Schlesinger, Edward. 1967. Letter to Joseph Papp, 27 November. *T-MSS 1993-028, Box II-79, F18. Joseph Papp/New York Shakespeare Festival Archives. Billy Rose Theatre Collection. New York Public Library for the Performing Arts.

Sokolow, Anna. 1967a. Letter to Gerald Freedman, 30 May. *T-MSS 1993-028, Box II-79, F7. Joseph Papp/New York Shakespeare Festival Archives. Billy Rose Theatre Collection. New York Public Library for the Performing Arts.

Sokolow, Anna. 1967b. Letter to Joseph Papp, 17 October. *T-MSS 1993-028, Box II-79, F7. Joseph Papp/New York Shakespeare Festival Archives. Billy Rose Theatre Collection. New York Public Library for the Performing Arts.

Unidentified clipping. Billy Rose Theatre Collection. MWEZ+n.c. 12, 591. New York Public Library for the Performing Arts.

Strange Brew

Radical Sexuality and *Che!*

John H. Houchin

O N 25 FEBRUARY 1970 the author, director, and cast of *Che!* had the dubious distinction of becoming the first theatre artists in more than thirty years to be convicted of obscenity in New York. The play—written by Lennox Raphael, a native Trinidadian, and directed by Ed Wode—contended that Latin American nations were victims of the United States' rapacious foreign policy. Specifically, the playwright depicted the last days of Che Guevera as a sexual nightmare in which Che is kidnapped and brought to the United States to satisfy the president's insatiable desire for sex and power. In order to impress the audience with this metaphor, four of the five-member cast performed nude for virtually the entire evening, participated in genital contact, and engaged in graphic simulations of hetero- and homosexual intercourse.[1]

Although *Che!* is a largely forgotten episode in theatre history, the discourse it prompted raised significant legal, ethical, and artistic issues regarding the limits of free expression and the degree of literalness that could be presented onstage. *Che!*'s defenders claimed that the production dealt with a current political topic and that the sexual enactments were valid political metaphors. Because it contained redeeming social value, it merited constitutional protection. The court ruled otherwise. Citing numerous precedents, Arthur Goldberg, who wrote the decision for the two-judge majority, concluded that in *Che!* the "sex was perva-

---

[1] The published version of *Che!* lists a sixth member of the cast. The program and subsequent newspaper articles indicate, however, that the cast numbered five.

sive but the politics elusive." Judge Goldberg stated that a fixed line separated constitutionally protected presentations from those that were obscene. *Che!* had crossed that line and therefore had forfeited its First Amendment rights (*People vs. Bercowitz* 1970).

Che! also sent shock waves through the theatre community. Playwrights anxiously debated whether Raphael merited their support. After all, *Che!* was transgressive and abusive. Such scripts would surely give the new national conservative majority, led by Richard Nixon, more ammunition in its battle to restrict the limits of expression. Actors were even more agitated. Since early 1968, stage nudity had been the topic of heated debate among performers. *Che!* introduced an even harsher prospect. Might actors be called on to depict intercourse in order to fulfill the demands of a script? Would actors now have to risk arrests and fines?

Although *Che!* was extreme, it was not an anomaly. Rather, it was part of the artistic harvest of the 1960s, violent years during which political and cultural radicals challenged the middle-class stranglehold on American morals and art. During the "turbulent sixties," normative society in the United States hardly seemed "normal" at all. Every person with access to a television could regularly view scenes of urban riots, campus demonstrations, love-ins, racially motivated beatings, funerals of assassinated leaders, and body bags from Vietnam. As race and the Vietnam War continued to suffuse the theatre of the late 1960s, cultural radicals turned increasingly to nudity and sexual displays to disrupt, debunk, and collapse the rigid middle-class moral and political structure.

This attack on the status quo had been greatly facilitated by a series of Supreme Court decisions that dramatically altered the legal definition of obscenity. Until the mid-twentieth century American courts supported the notion that if any portion of a book or play corrupted "sensitive or susceptible" people, the entire work could be regarded as obscene (Wagman 1991, 202–6).[2] In 1957 the Supreme Court radically altered this criterion by agreeing to review *Roth vs. United States,* a profoundly important case. Samuel Roth, a publisher of adult books and magazines, had been convicted of distributing obscene materials. Although the Court upheld the verdict, the case became famous for the opinion written by Justice William Brennan. To be obscene, he ruled, expression had to be "utterly without redeeming social importance." He further ruled that material could only be judged obscene if (1) the "average person," (2) "applying contemporary community standards,"

---

[2]This legal opinion was largely based on an English legal decision known as *Regina vs. Hicklin.*

(3) would find that the "dominant theme of the material taken as a whole . . . appeals to prurient interests" (Wagman 1991, 205).

Although *Roth* liberalized the definition of obscenity, the role of sex in middle-class American society was not commonly debated until the 1960s. On 11 May 1960, the Food and Drug Administration approved G. D. Searl's application to produce the world's first oral contraceptive, thereby permanently liberating the sex act from conception (Baritz 1982, 229–30). From the day oral contraception was introduced millions of Americans were intrigued by a discourse that attempted to define the purpose of sex both inside and outside of marriage. Sexual materials flooded the marketplace. Aided by more federal court decisions, dozens of full-length feature films depicting all manner of erotica were released during the 1960s.[3] *Human Sexual Response,* by William H. Masters and Virginia E. Johnson, was published in April 1966 and within one week became a national best-seller. By the mid-1970s Hugh Hefner's *Playboy* magazine reached in excess of six million readers. His counterpart, Helen Gurley Brown, transformed *Cosmopolitan* into a female variant of *Playboy.* Sex, she maintained, was a tool and, like money, should be used for personal benefit (D'Emilio and Freedman 1988, 303–5).

The erotic movies and magazines of the 1960s prompted knee-jerk warnings about declining morals, but nudity and transgressive sexuality in live performance incited more volatile responses. The experience of reading a novel or magazine is private, and graphic representation is unnecessary for enjoyment. Sexual adventures depicted on film, although they may be realistic, are nonetheless removed in time and space from the audience. Their impact is technologically mediated, and they are clearly designed as a fantasy in which the viewer participates imaginatively. Sexuality and nudity in theatre transpires within an entirely different set of conditions. Actors, even when fully clothed, inhabit an emotionally charged, precariously ambiguous world. Theatre is executed by living, breathing humans who are obviously present and, theoretically, available. As Richard Schechner stated in *Public Domain,* "stage performance is always on the verge of tumbling back into the real world" (1969a, 141).

Given the convulsive political climate and the national obsession with

---

[3]For a thorough treatment of censored films see Edward de Grazia and Roger K. Newman, *Banned Films: Movies, Censors, and the First Amendment* (New York: R. R. Bowker, 1982). Some of the most famous (or notorious, depending on one's point of view) of these were *Women of the World* (Italy 1963); *491 Loma* (Sweden 1964); *A Stranger Knocks* (Denmark 1963); *I, a Woman* (Sweden 1965); *I Am Curious— Yellow* (Sweden 1965); *Blow-Up* (United States 1966); and *Chelsea Girls* (United States 1966).

issues of sexuality, it was just a matter of time before these two conditions were linked within the paradoxical world of theatrical performance in an equation that produced an excessively unstable chemistry. As with most historical trends, a fixed starting point is elusive, but one of the earliest examples of this type of presentation was Michael McClure's *The Beard*, which opened on 24 October 1967 at the Evergreen Theatre on East Eleventh Street. In the play two characters, "Billy the Kid" and "Jean Harlow," engage in a fiercely antagonistic, Strindbergian sexual battle. There is no action in the Aristotelian sense, and the dialogue, which is ritualistically repetitive, is littered with expletives and sexual allusions. It was the final scene, however, that caused the most furor. With Jean seated in Billy's chair, he gradually placed his head between her thighs and began to simulate oral sex. New York critics concentrated on the pop art significance of the characters but delicately avoided mentioning the obvious sexual display at the end of the play.

Outside of the permissive confines of New York, *The Beard* and numerous other countercultural productions were treated as if they were invading armies. A student production of McClure's play at California State University at Fullerton in November 1967 prompted a legislative inquiry into the patriotism of the college administration (Professor's). *Hair* introduced Broadway audiences to the rock counterculture of the sixties in April 1968. When, however, it was ready to open in Boston in February 1970, the Essex County district attorney threatened to arrest the entire cast if certain scenes were not deleted.[4] In June 1969 *Dionysus in 69,* a contemporary reworking of *The Bacchae,* was presented by Richard Schechner and his company, the Performance Group. It featured a chorus of nude and/or partially nude actors who staged an orgiastic birth ritual and interacted with the audience, which had also been invited to disrobe. During the winter of 1968–69, the company toured western and midwestern universities. Reviewers of the University of Colorado production called it a "poisonous puss of four-lettered words and a senseless display of nudity." After a performance at the University of Michigan in January 1969, Schechner and his cast were arrested for indecent exposure (Schechner 1969b; *Detroit News*). The Living Theatre's *Paradise Now* also generated intense controversy. When the production premiered in New Haven in September 1968, Julian Beck, Judith Malina, and their company, clad only in bikinis and G-strings, led the audience into the streets of the city to lay claim to

---

[4] The producers of *Hair* appealed and the Supreme Judicial Court of Massachusetts consented to allow the production to open intact.

"Paradise." They were immediately arrested for indecent exposure. The Living Theatre subsequently encountered police opposition in Philadelphia, Minneapolis, and Los Angeles.[5]

The media never seemed to tire of feature stories examining the depiction of the "new morality." Scores of articles in *McCall's, U.S. News and World Report, New Republic,* and *Christian Century* reviewed the pervasiveness of sex in contemporary entertainments. Provocative exposés entitled "Sex and the Arts: Explosive Scene," "The Nude Brood," "The Naked American," "The Naked Craze," "The Naked Stage," and "Sex as a Spectator Sport" appeared routinely in national periodicals. The public was also greeted with multipage examinations of nudity in performance, complete with extensive photo documentation, in *Time, Newsweek,* and *Life.* Throughout 1968 and 1969 the discourse was even more heated in New York, with literally thousands of column inches devoted to this one topic.

However, opponents of permissive sexual displays, supported by a president who had promised to restore national decency, had begun to organize. The galvanizing incident occurred in March of 1969, when Jim Morrison of "The Doors" was arrested in Miami for exposing himself and using obscene language at a concert attended by thousands of teenagers. In response a Miami teen, with support from the VFW and local churches, organized a "Rally for Decency," which was attended by over thirty thousand people, mostly flag-waving youth.[6] The idea caught on, and similar rallies took place in Indianapolis, Cincinnati, Minneapolis, Birmingham, and Austin (Morals). Self-generated groups calling themselves Citizens for Decent Literature sprang up around the nation to police publishers. By July over 135 antipornography bills were pending before the House Judiciary Committee (Sex).

When *Che!* opened on 22 March of that year at the Free Store Theatre on Cooper Square, it added more fuel to a very hot fire. To Raphael, at least, his project was a legitimate revolutionary activity. "The duty of the revolutionary is to make the revolution, regardless of how indefinite the struggle. And writing is revolution when done in the interest of the revolution," he stated in his "Foreplay" to *Che!* (1969, xiii).

---

[5]Although these three productions encountered the most legal opposition, several others generated a significant amount of controversy. *Tom Paine* premiered at Ellen Stewart's La Mama Theatre in March 1968. *Futz!*, by Rochelle Owens, opened in June 1968; *Oh! Calcutta!* in June 1968; *Beclch* in December 1968; *Sweet Eros* in November 1969; and *The Young Master Dante* in December 1969.

[6]President Nixon responded by sending a personal letter of congratulations to Mike Levesque, the organizer of the rally.

In the introduction to *Che!*, written after his arrest but before his conviction, he attempted to describe how he had integrated his personal and political philosophy into his play:

> All roads lead to the jungle or thru it. . . . The jungle introduces us to ourselves, makes us relevant in the struggle to become functional unto ourselves, then to others as we overcome. . . . My attitude toward theatre is the same. It must do something for us, help us along to knowing ourselves and action! Life is the supreme fantasy. And effective theatre is a mirror without cracks, straight to you. . . . You confront the mirror, you see yourself for what you are. . . . If armed revolutionary victory (liberation) issues from the barrel of a gun, then this disarming revolution of the theatre issues from our bodies. (1969, viii)

Although Raphael's prose style may leave something to be desired, he apparently believed that he was involved in a socially relevant project.

Although the script itself contains very few stage directions, the list of indictments and the photo documentation clearly indicated that Raphael and Wode intended to produce the most audacious, sexually explicit show ever to be seen in New York. Of the six cast members, only Breakstone Fearless (Movie Director), who appeared infrequently, and Chili Dilly (Son of King Kong), who provided guitar accompaniment (at least as far as can be surmised from the script), remained clothed. The other characters—Che, Mayfang (Intelligence Agent), the president of the United States, and Sister of Mercy (Viciously Delicious Angelspy)—initiated most of the action and were either scantily dressed or virtually nude. For example, when the actor playing the president arrived at the theatre opening night, he emerged from his taxi with his toenails painted red and adorned in nothing but a red, white, and blue sash and top hat. The actress portraying Sister of Mercy (Viciously Delicious Angelspy) wore only a rosary around her neck and bikini bottoms for most of the performance. She quoted Pope John XXIII and Augustine and spoke lines such as "COME ALL YE FAITHFUL," "Oh purple fuck of immaculate fruition," "My box is sweet," and "This is better than my Jesus Christ." There were several instances of hetero- and homosexual genital contact, simulated oral and anal sex, mimed defecation, and a large clear plastic penis was periodically displayed (Raphael 1969, 163).[7]

The 138-page script virtually defies interpretation and can best be de-

---

[7]The full list of indictments is published as an appendix in the Contact Books edition of the script.

scribed as an accumulation of stream-of-consciousness one-liners that link political aggression with sexual sadomasochism. The following excerpt is typical of the dialogue:

> PRESIDENT: Are you at peace with your ultimate innocence?
> SISTER: You puzzle me.
> MAYFANG: Get thee behind his ass, and stop shaking.
> SISTER: OOOOOOOOOOOOoooooooooooo!
> MAYFANG: You're going to excite him.
> PRESIDENT: She will illumine my excitement.
> SISTER: My clitoris cannot stand this jive political satori.
> PRESIDENT: You do have a fine piece of ass for a Sister. (Raphael 1969, 105)

There are virtually no stage directions and most of the action was only loosely connected to the language. There were virtually no specific geopolitical references because sexual activity was meant to signify general American foreign aggression.

As soon as *Che!* opened for previews, complaints were lodged with the police. Amos S. Basel, judge for the Criminal Court, having been apprised of the sexual nature of the production, attended the opening performance. The *New York Post* reported that after the curtain he left the theatre, briefly discussed the play with police officers who had been stationed outside the theatre, and immediately signed arrest warrants. Police entered the theatre and arrested the cast of five and the five-member production staff (*Che!* Cast). Each was arraigned that night on charges of lewdness, consensual sodomy, and obscenity. Their attorney, Arthur Turco, a member of William Kunstler's defense team, accused Judge Basil of prejudice, claiming that "it was his [Judge Basil's] conscience which was shocked" (Actors and Author of *Che!* Are Charged). Raphael promised to reopen the production in spite of police harassment but announced the next day that *Che!* would temporarily close. On 27 March 1969 Kunstler himself argued for a restraining order in Federal District Court. He asserted that the play dealt with "political realities in sexual terms" and that it did not appeal exclusively to prurient interests. The court disagreed and refused to issue an injunction (Bid). On 7 May a fifty-four-count indictment was handed down. That night the company reopened an altered version of the production, which had eliminated all genital contact. These deletions, in the mind of the deputy police inspector who saw the performance, were insufficient, and the cast was again arrested (Actors and Author of *Che!* Are Charged).

There were some who praised Raphael. Ross Wetzsteon wrote in the

Village Voice that the author had fused the sexual, artistic, and political revolution in one effort (quoted in "Where Do We Go?"). The *East Village Other* called the play an "intricately choreographed coming together and falling asunder of forms, emotions, rites and ideas—at the end, the stillness and the sobs are unbearably lovely" (Decomposition). The foreman of a demolition crew interviewed in the *New York Post* was more blunt: "Look they got those movies up on 42nd Street. And some hotels got madams and everything else," he claimed. "You see, there's degeneracy in everybody. I don't care even the President of the United States. At least these people don't hide. They bring it out" (*Che! Dirty?*).

For the most part, however, *Che!* met with fierce opposition. An indignant editor for the *New York Post* fumed that *Che!* and other shows of the same ilk were the "pervading curse of our lives" (Looking). The *New York Times* editorialized: "Explicit portrayal on the stage of sexual intercourse is the final step in the erosion of taste and subtlety in the theatre. It reduces actors to mere exhibitionists, turns audiences into voyeurs and debases sexual relationships almost to the level of prostitution. It is difficult to see any great principle of civil liberties involved when persons indulging themselves on stage in this kind of peep show activity are arrested for 'public lewdness and obscenity'" (Beyond). *Newsweek* called *Che!* "a squalid series of loveless fornications and related sexual gymnastics, performed in the nude and reminiscent of nothing so much as the kind of peep show that used to flourish in Port Said during the reign of the late King Farouk" (Morals).

Che! went to trial in January 1970, and the question of whether intercourse actually occurred during the performance became a central issue. The *Village Voice* asserted that the sex scenes were not simulated but real, "depending upon the mood of the cast" (The Theatre). A CBS reporter also testified that Raphael told him that "the actors had been told they were at liberty to perform any sex act on stage at any time, if they felt spontaneously that actual sex would enhance the realism of their performance (*People vs. Bercowitz* 1970). However, Larry Bercowitz, who played Che, asserted that he and Mary Anne Shelly, who performed Sister of Mercy, rehearsed their eight-minute intercourse scene so thoroughly that people thought we were really "doing it" (*Che!* in Court).

The trial brought out a number of expert witnesses who testified for and against the production. David Merrick fumed that the performance he saw was "patently offensive," containing all "combinations of physical contact," which he found "prurient, lewd, and vulgar." He said that the playwright was without any talent whatsoever and should seek vocational guidance. He concluded by saying that New York theatre was essentially going to the dogs. "I love theatre, but I fear the New York theatre is getting a reputation that is bad for the drama. . . . I do not feel sex is a spectator sport. The public portrayal of nudity is objectionable. . . . [I]t's thrown in for box office" (David Merrick). Clive Barnes, on the other hand, testified that the play was essentially political, and although it was of low quality, it still retained redeeming social value and should not be closed.

On 25 February 1970 a two-to-one decision rendered by a panel of judges of the Manhattan Criminal Court was clearly intended to restrict the use of sexual display in a live performance. The cast, producer, playwright, and set designer were found guilty "of participating in an obscene performance which predominantly appealed and pandered to prurient interest" (*People vs. Bercowitz* 1970). The majority decision maintained that *Che!* went beyond the "customary limits of candor by presenting profanity, filth, defecation, masochism, sadism, masturbation, nudity, copulation, sodomy and other deviant sexual intercourse" (ibid.). Judge Goldberg rejected Raphael's argument that the sexual content of the play was identical to its political message. He stated, "The pretended political content of the play was elusive, both in performance of the play and in its commercial exploitation, and that the whole play and performance had no redeeming social value" (ibid.).

Particularly crucial was the aspect of commercial exploitation. Judge Goldberg pointed to the fact that tickets cost ten dollars, the most expensive on off-off-Broadway. Moreover, he noted that the production had been "advertised daily in leading New York City newspapers including the *New York Times*" (ibid.). These efforts, he maintained, amounted to pandering, a charge that proved profit, not political protest, had motivated the production. Nor did he accept the producers' contention that *Che!* was merely part of the radical off-off-Broadway theatrical movement. He countered that "standards of public acceptance and morality" cannot "be established by a few commercially inspired producers who try to see how far they can go." Finally, he added an ominous note that dealt with another line. He admitted that the Supreme Court had recently established "standards of prurience, expression, and redeeming social value in books and other written material"; the Court, however, had yet to decide that the same standards can be applied to live performances. "What may be found in the novel to be of redeeming social value," he claimed, "may not at all suffice to protect a live performance containing prurient and patently offensive material" (*People vs. Bercowitz* 1970). Five who were convicted were unconditionally released. The others were given the option of spending sixty days in jail or paying fines ranging from $500 to $1000 (8 in *Che!*).

After the cast of *Che!* was arrested, the theatre community of New York underwent an intense reevaluation of its artistic and ethical standards. For playwrights the *Che!* case was a polarizing event. The joint councils of the Dramatists Guild and the Author's League hastily met and agreed to issue an open letter to Mayor John Lindsay. In it they maintained that closing the play prior to a judicial decision amounted to censorship by intimidation and seriously endangered the freedom of expression in theatre (Letter).

Once the issue of actual intercourse was raised, however, some members began to vacillate. In a meeting called in early April to discuss censorship, Frank Gilroy, president of the Dramatists Guild, claimed that theatre was about mimesis, not reality: "[F]or me, as long as things are depicted—in other words, mimed—I can accept any extreme. I don't care what's said, and I don't care what's acted. But when you move into the area of the actual act, then suddenly something in me calls a halt" (Discussion 5).

Those who defended *Che!* skirted the conundrum of reality vs. mimesis and focused on the larger issue of freedom of expression. Jerome Weidman challenged his colleagues: "Do we, as an organization, approve or disapprove of censorship in any form whatsoever? . . . It seems to me, no price is too high to pay for a free press, even if the price is allowing something like *Che!* to be exhibited to those people who are willing to go to a box office and pay for it" (Discussion 7–8).

The problems that stage nudity presented for performers were more immediate. Actors were continually asked to infuse their characterizations with intimate and sometimes painful personal experiences. Now they were being told that nudity was the ultimate form of personal disclosure. An unidentified actor succinctly defined his dilemma in a *Newsweek* interview: "It's real, it's you and there's no place to hide" (Naked Stage). Actress Monica Evans expressed the belief that appearing nude onstage was antithetical to the process of acting. "I kept thinking, that wouldn't be me the actress," she said, "that would be me. . . . [N]udity invades the rights of a human being. My body belongs to me—that's my private life, my personal territory" (Actresses 28). Sally Kirkland, whom the *Times* claimed had "virtually made a career of nudity," took a totally different attitude: "I have no hang-up about nudity. I think the human body is beautiful and as long as I feel that what I'm doing is artistic, I have no objection to appearing nude" (ibid.). Judyann Elder, who frequently performed with the Negro En-

semble Company, called stage nudity a "white hang-up" that "is not
one step above those girlie magazine stores and movie houses on 42nd
Street. . . . For the actor, this is nothing short of debilitating and ex-
hausting to his artistic individuality" (To Be).

Although the issue of stage nudity was clearly troubling and divisive
for actors, the explicitness of *Che!* altered the trajectory of that discourse. Prior to *Che!* actors discussed stage nudity in terms of personal
and artistic integrity. After the cast was arrested, the discussion included
issues of abuse and criminal prosecution. On 24 April 1969, 160 members of Actor's Equity petitioned the union to address the issue of exploitation (160 in Equity). One of the Equity petitioners maintained
that performers were asked to undress before auditioning or before they
even knew anything about the play. They had no way of knowing if
they were actually being considered for a role or were simply providing
entertainment for a producer and his friends. Auditioners were also
asked to improvise hetero- and homosexual love scenes, and males were
even asked to arouse themselves. In what was perhaps a direct reference
to *Che!*, the spokesperson also noted that actors were now being asked
to perform certain acts in the theatre that were illegal and that there
was no reason why individuals who had "already made sacrifices to remain in this profession should be asked to risk arrest and imprisonment
to boot" (To Be).

Equity responded by issuing a set of guidelines aimed at protecting
its members. It stipulated that an actor could be asked to remove his
or her clothes only after the singing, dancing, and acting auditions had
been completed. It required that an Equity official had to be present
on such occasions, which, in turn, could be attended only by recognized
producers, directors, and choreographers. Finally, it stated that actors
had to be informed in writing if the script called for nudity or any
simulated sex acts before contracts were signed. Under this policy a producer had to indemnify a performer in case of arrest and furnish all
fines, bail, and legal fees (Actors Equity).

It is entirely possible that *Che!* even influenced the final shape of *Oh!
Calcutta!*, Kenneth Tynan's erotic romp that began previews in May
1969. A series of sketches, songs, and dances performed wholly or
partially nude, *Oh! Calcutta!* simply reified middle-class heterosexual
fantasies. Having witnessed what happened to *Che!*, producer Hillard
Elkins took extraordinary efforts to distance himself from radical theatre. In an unprecedented step he invited various city officials to previews
and pruned scenes in accordance with their advice. "We are not trying
to make a revolution," he remarked. "I am simply trying to produce
an entertainment in the erotic area in the best possible taste. We do

not wish to offend, we want to amuse and we're looking for all the help we can get" (City Officials). Even Senator Jacob Javitts, Rudolf Nureyev, and Jerome Robbins were asked for their opinions (Tynan 1988, 283).[8]

Although the dramatic merits of *Che!* are obviously debatable, this short-lived countercultural production was nonetheless significant. It vividly supported Judith Lynn Hannah's claim that the body is "contested terrain" (Hannah 1998, 51). As the supporters of *Che!* had held, transgressive sexual displays were laden with political implications. The state, through Judge Goldberg's decision, clearly indicated that it had a vested interest in how and under what circumstances the human body could be displayed. Moreover, the theatre community was forced to engage in a dialectic that pitted freedom of expression against rights of privacy. And although *Che!* disappeared, the discourse that it generated is still with us.

Works Cited

"Actors and Author of *Che!* Are Charged with Obscenity." 1969. *New York Times* 16 March, p. 37.

"Actors and Author of *Che!* Arrested after Performance." 1969. *New York Times*, 8 May, p. 33

Actors Equity Sets Rules for Nudity in Theatre." 1969. *New York Times*, 20 May, p. 41.

"Actresses Talk about Onstage Nudity." 1969. *New York Times*, 17 February, p. 28.

Baritz, Loren. *The Good Life: The Meaning of Success for the American*. New York: Harper and Row, 1982.

"Beyond the (Garbage) Pale." 1969. *New York Times*, 1 April, p. 46.

"Bid to Reopen *Che!* Fails in U.S. Court." 1969. *New York Times*, 28 March, p. 38.

"*Che!* Cast Vows to Carry On and Take It Off." 1969. *New York Post*, 25 March, p. 24.

"*Che!* Dirty? Not So Says a Man in Street." 1969. *New York Post*, 27 March, p. 12.

"*Che!* in Court: Evidence? Well!" 1969. *New York Post*, 15 July (clipping). New York Public Library at Lincoln Center.

"City Officials Consulting with *Oh! Calcutta!* Staff." 1969. *New York Times*, 24 May, p. 27.

"David Merrick, at Cast's Trial, Assails *Che!* as Without Value." 1970. *New York Times*, 20 January, p. 36.

---

[8]Tynan believed the final result was a tawdry burlesque and wanted his name removed from the credits three days before the production opened.

"Decomposition." 1969. *East Village Other*, 14 March (clipping). New York
 Public Library at Lincoln Center.

D'Emilio, John, and Estelle B. Freedman. 1988. *Intimate Matter: A History of
 Sexuality in America*. New York: Harper and Row.

Detroit News. 1969. 27 January, p. 1.

"A Discussion of Censorship and the Case of *Che!*." 1969. *Dramatists Guild
 Quarterly* (spring): 5+.

"8 in *Che!* Are Found Guilty of Obscenity." 1970. *New York Times*, 26 February,
 p. 30.

Hannah, Judith Lynn. 1998. "Undressing the First Amendment and Corseting
 the Striptease Dancer." *Drama Review* 42 (summer): 38–64.

"Letter to John V. Lindsay and District Attorney Frank S. Hogan." 1969.
 Dramatists Guild Quarterly (spring): 8.

"Looking at Obscenity." 1969. *New York Post*, 26 March (clipping). New York
 Public Library at Lincoln Center.

"Morals: Backlash." 1969. *Newsweek*, 17 April, p. 31.

"The Naked Stage." 1969. *Newsweek*, 3 March, p. 80.

"160 in Equity Ask Union to Redress Nudity Grievance." 1969. *New York Times*,
 24 April, p. 38.

"The People of the State of New York vs. Larry Bercowitz, et. al. 1970. Criminal
 Court of the City of New York, 25 February.

"Professor's Dismissal Demanded over 'Beard.'" 1968. *Los Angeles Times*, 26
 January, sec. 1, p. 1.

Raphael, Lennox. 1969. *Che!* New York: Contact Books.

Schechner, Richard. 1969a. *Public Domain*. New York: Bobbs-Merrill.

———. 1969b. "Speculations on Radicalism, Sexuality, and Performance."
 Drama Review 13 (summer): 93–94.

"Sex as a Spectator Sport." 1969. *Time*, 11 July, p. 61.

"The Theatre of Arousal: Dramatis Interruptus." 1969. *Village Voice*, 25 March
 (clipping). New York Public Library at Lincoln Center.

"To Be or Not to Be Nude—That Is the Question." 1969. *New York Times*, 22
 June, sec. 11, p. 10.

Tynan, Kathleen. 1988. *The Life of Kenneth Tynan*. London: Methuen.

Wagman, Robert J. 1991. *The First Amendment Book*. New York: Pharos Books.

"Where Do We Go from *Che!*?" 1969. *New York Times*, 4 May, sec. D, p. 3.

Experiments in Deconstruction-Reconstruction

Working Methods of Parma's Compagnia del Collettivo in Its Shakespearean Trilogy

Stanley Vincent Longman

In 1900 the government of the city of Parma, Italy, built a theatre, calling it Teatro Due (or Theatre Two) to distinguish it from Parma's prestigious opera house, which, of course, is "teatro uno." Teatro Due was the theatre building that eventually housed the Compagnia del Collettivo. From the beginning the Teatro Due sponsored yearly international festivals featuring new, experimental theatre work. Called the Festival di Teatro Universitario, it brought together student-artists from universities throughout Europe to witness the work of such experimental companies and artists as the Living Theatre, Cricot 2, Charles Marowitz, and others. It was in that context that the Compagnia del Collettivo emerged, for its founding members—Gigi Dall'Aglio, Roberto Abbati, Gianpaolo Bocelli, and Walter Le Moli—were all students from the University of Parma and members of its theatre club, the Centro Universitario Teatrale. The experience of helping to arrange and then attend these performances strongly influenced the founders (Shakespeare Project 1982). Indeed, after the Italian university theatre organizations became moribund, the people of the Collettivo continued the festival as Teatro Festival Parma to the present day.

The spirit of the Compagnia del Collettivo grew directly out of the upheavals of 1968, a spirit that was still very much alive in 1971, the year of the company's creation. They, of course, joined in the distrust of power and authority and in the insistence on digging at the roots of our shared humanity that came with the 1968 uprisings. Similarly, the company sought to create a genuine "theatre collective" in which repertory decisions, rehearsal processes, and management were all accomplished by mutual endeavor. Company members wanted to produce performances responsive to the times, performances that would awaken awareness of the world we occupy. They saw theatre in dialectical terms, as capable of exposing through the microcosm of the stage the forces that impinge on the macrocosm of society, and they hoped to create in the audience a sense of synthesis, a realization of alternatives to the social and political order. The stage, in their terms, is an open ground shared by actors and spectators and embodying actions, events, rituals that can so absorb one's being as to cause intense engagement and even visceral response (Dall'Aglio 1989).

One means for accomplishing this engagement and response consists of transforming well known legends, novels, plays, histories, and chronicles into new spectacles that astonish, partly because of their strangeness and partly because of their sometimes uncanny resemblance to our own times. Another means derives from the Collettivo's dispensing with elaborate scenic expression in favor of a bare stage or even a shared space occupied by actors and audience alike—environmental theatre of the sort propounded by Antonin Artaud and practiced by Jerzy Grotowski, Richard Schechner, Eugenio Barba, Joseph Chaikin, and others. In such instances the tendency is to play on the unique quality of the theatrical medium—its ability to create a direct encounter between performer and spectator. Examples of similar efforts abound in the second half of the twentieth century. One thinks, for example, of Peter Weiss's *Marat/Sade,* Heinar Kipphardt's *In the Case of J. Robert Oppenheimer,* Ariane Mnouchkine's *1789,* Luca Ronconi's *Orlando Furioso,* Schechner's *Dionysus in 69,* Grotowski's *The Constant Prince,* Charles Marowitz's *Hamlet: A Collage,* or, for that matter, Heiner Müller's *Hamletmachine.* Common to all these, also, is the device of fragmentation through which events are set apart in episodes or mere moments; characters are split into two or more agents; an event is undercut by a simultaneous one; or focus is shared between two or more activities onstage.

All of these characteristics appear in the work of the Collettivo. What makes its work unusual is its practice of collaborative deconstruction of play texts and improvisatory reconstruction. In place of the "image-making" of the fifties and sixties—which used television, ad campaigns, propaganda, and slogans to portray the world as self-contained and unalterable—the Collettivo attempts to create spectacles that are themselves "plays in the making." The audience sees the stage play as stage play, witnesses the improvisation at work, the exposed lighting instruments, actors assuming and dropping character, and props stored and brought out. This is "metatheatre" in Lionel Abel's terminology, with the stage no longer self-contained by sustained illusion but rather open, aware of itself and its audience, deliberate in its allusions and referents (Abel 1963, 105–7). Through this approach the Collettivo sought to place theatre in the midst of our times, as a social and artistic institution operating in a society composed of people whose senses, sensibilities, and insights can be engaged in the act of theatre. The Collettivo's techniques of taking a text apart, examining it, exploring it, improvising on it, and rebuilding it into a performance with an essentially new text are all calculated to reinforce this metatheatrical concept.

The Collettivo has produced scores of plays over the past three decades, but they take special pride in those that are "company developed." From the beginning they worked many months (and occasionally up to two years) on a project of deconstruction and reconstruction. This practice began during 1971 and 1972 with *Il re è nudo* (The king is naked), based on the story of the emperor's new clothes. Since then, the Collettivo has developed many similar projects, most notably *Turandot* (1973–74, based on Gozzi and Brecht), variations on Eduardo de Filippo's *Il figlio di Pulcinella* (The son of Pulcinella) the following year, and Dario Fo's *La colpa è sempre del diavolo* (It's always the Devil's fault), the latter two done in collaboration with their actor/manager creators. The company has also developed productions based on Rabelais' *Gargantua and Pantagruel* and Jules Verne's *Fantastic Voyage* (Shakespeare Project 1982).

In light of these precedents it was perhaps inevitable that the Collettivo would eventually turn to producing Shakespeare in a contemporary spirit. They chose to combine and revise four plays—*Hamlet, Macbeth, Henry IV, Part 1*, and *Henry IV, Part 2*—into a trilogy with a distinctive progression to its structure. The Shakespearean stage itself tends toward the metatheatrical, often calling attention to itself and referring in one way or another to the larger world beyond the stage. In this tradition the Collettivo took from Shakespeare three quotations that served as signposts of this *teatrum mundi:* From *Hamlet,* "The play is the thing" (2.2.602); from *Macbeth,* "Life's but a walking shadow, a poor player / that struts and frets his hour upon the stage / and then is heard no more" (5.5.26–29); and from *Henry IV, Part 2,* Falstaff's challenge: "Shall we have a play extempore?" (2.4.273).

Strong influences on the Collettivo's thinking came from the writings of Antonin Artaud, Bertolt Brecht, and, most immediately, Jan Kott (Dall'Aglio 1989). Artaud's arguments for a "theatre of cruelty" that would awaken the deepest and darkest promptings of the human spirit and his case against fixed, rigid masterpieces have much to do with the open and direct stagings of violence and intrigue that characterize the plays developed by the Collettivo. Artaud called for a common ground between spectacle and spectator to create a direct communication with an audience "placed in the middle of the action . . . engulfed and physically affected by it" (1958, 96).

The use of legends and history in the context of a frankly theatrical stage characterizes Brecht's dramaturgy in keeping with his principle of *Verfremdungseffekt,* whereby audience members are to be kept mindful of their own world as they witness the strange, "historified" world of the play. Brecht called for a theatre that chose not to *represent* the world as a closed, fixed, unchanging reality but rather to *present* it as open, engaging, and in flux. Its very mutable nature can awaken in the audience a desire to effect change. The Collettivo was very alive to these ideas, especially as they could be translated into principles of acting and the *gestus* (Dall'Aglio 1983, 100–101). Curiously, Brecht dismissed Shakespeare as one whose worlds were fixed and immutable: "The theatre as we know it shows the structure of society (represented on stage) as incapable of being influenced by society (in the auditorium). Shakespeare's great solitary figures, bearing on their breast the star of their fate, carry through with irresistible force their futile and deadly outbursts; they prepare their own downfall; life, not death, becomes obscene as they collapse; the catastrophe is beyond criticism" (1964, 189).

Although Jan Kott agrees that Shakespeare's worlds have a fixed and immutable quality, he finds in them a capacity for electric interaction with audiences. He sees the Shakespearean stage serving beautifully to contain a particular world while incorporating those around it, including the audience and ultimately the force of all history. Kott draws a distinction between two interpretations of "dramatic history." The first views history as rational and progressive; the other sees it as meaningless, as standing still, or as endlessly repeating its cruel cycle as an elemental force. Kott views Shakespeare as presenting this latter vision in which history is a "Grand Mechanism," a machine whose cogs are great lords and hired assassins catching its people up in violence, cruelty, and treason and sending great rulers down roads to power that are ultimately roads to death (Kott 1966, 38). But the Grand Mechanism is not just cruel; it is also a tragic farce (40). This, on close analysis, is not so far removed from Brecht's vision of the world. Kott later notes that

Shakespeare was very fond of comparing life to the theatre. It is a comparison that goes back to ancient times, but it was Shakespeare who endowed it with depth and clarity. 'Teatrum mundi' is neither tragic nor comic. It just employs tragic and comic actors. What is the tyrant's part in that theatre? Richard [III] is impersonal like history itself. He is the consciousness and mastermind of the Grand Mechanism. He puts in motion the steam-roller of history, and later is crushed by it. Richard is not even cruel. Psychology does not apply to him. He is just history, one of its ever-repeating characters. (53–54)

This is also the spirit of the Collettivo's Shakespearean trilogy. The history portrayed in the plays—plays that are themselves part of history—is a history that is ever present with us. The Collettivo sought to "rediscover" Shakespeare in contemporary terms, which accounts for its adoption of a dialectic framework, of a deliberate theatricalism with blatant character transformations, of anachronistic invention, and of mixed tone.

The performances almost always begin with a statement from Luis Borges, quoting Miguel Cervantes and Louis-Nicolas Ménard. It is a challenging statement that provokes reflection on the weight and effect we experience by our place in history:

> The relationship between the words of Cervantes and those of Ménard is more than revealing. The former, for example, wrote (in *Don Quixote,* Part I, Chapter VIII): "Truth, whose mother is History, emulates time, itself the depository of the actions and witness of the past, the example and news of the present, and warning of the future." Written in the seventeenth century, written out of the genius of Cervantes this enumeration is a mere rhetorical eulogy to history. By contrast, Ménard writes, "Truth, whose mother is History, emulates time, itself the depository of the actions and witness of the past, the example and news of the present, and warning of the future." History as the mother of Truth: the idea is marvelous. Ménard, a contemporary of William James, does not see history as the search for reality, but rather as its source. Historical truth, for him, is not what happens but what we judge to happen. (quoted in Dall'Aglio 1983, 99).

The import of the quotation lies in its singling out the relative or pragmatic nature of historical truth. What was true for one epoch may shift drastically for another. Although the fundamental facts and issues may remain, their interpretations may fluctuate wildly. Meanwhile, history moves on in its own blind, inexorable way.

There may be no better illustration of this than in Shakespeare, whose works constantly renew themselves with successive epochs and interpretations. Tying *Hamlet, Macbeth,* and *Henry IV* together was a concept of a continual dialectic whereby the action grows as response to the disjointedness of the world. Hamlet's Denmark has something out of joint and rotten in its nature, and his play explores his putting it right. Macbeth's murky Scotland is infused with words and prophesies that spark actions that undermine any sense of human cohesion or continuity. And finally, Falstaff and Hal confront the world in drastically different ways—the one with a hedonism that turns its back on the world at large for the sake of indulgence, the other ultimately coming to terms pragmatically (if not a little sadly) with the forces that operate in the political and social arenas. These of course are issues present in the original texts of the plays, but in the hands of the Collettivo, the texts constituted a pretext for elaboration of a richly varied, intensely theatrical experience that existed both out of time and in the contemporary moment.

Theatre, not surprisingly, is an ideal place to examine this phenomenon of mankind in the context of time and space because theatre is both what we perceive now, in the immediate moment, and what was perceived in times past. It has the transitory sense of life itself. Consequently, what we count as reality (in history as well as in theatrical performance) becomes a matter of perception. Dall'Aglio quotes Artaud to the effect that contemporary audiences may fail to relate to Oedipus not because they are stupid or uneducated but because they no longer perceive reality as Sophocles perceived it (1983, 100). And yet that does not mean that Sophocles, or Shakespeare, has nothing to offer us. It simply is a matter of finding a common meeting ground. Hence the need, as Jan Kott suggested, to rediscover these texts by taking them apart, exploring them in pieces and reassembling them as performance. Except in the most literal sense, the text does not disappear. It reappears in a new and more revealing guise.

The Collettivo's dialectical method operates on several levels. It characterizes the company's working methods, with Shakespeare's texts serving as thesis; the workshop deconstruction and improvisation as antithesis; and performance as synthesis. There is a progression moving from the box-like staging of *Hamlet*, to the cinematic imagery of *Macbeth*, to the three-sided environmental arrangement for *Henry IV*. There is also in the plays a progression in the use of "metacharacters" who ultimately become more abstract and forceful. Moreover, the dialectic is drawn among the plays themselves: *Hamlet* serving as thesis; *Macbeth* antithesis; and *Henry IV* as synthesis. As Luigi Allegri has noted, in perhaps the most thorough investigation of the Collettivo's Shakespearean trilogy, Hamlet is the intellectual in crisis, one who in "a moment of rebellion *a la* 1968, throws away his books crying 'no more philosophy!' but who nevertheless remains intellectual" (1983, 14). That spirit informs his every action: he responds to a world emptied of meaning and purpose, the world of "rotten Denmark," by seeking out a gesture, an action, something that can put it right. Hamlet takes to creating spectacle—a spectacle of himself in his antic disposition and a literal spectacle in the mousetrap play he has the players mount before the king. The audience is frankly acknowledged. Hamlet creates other spectacles inside the spectacle. Even Ophelia's madness becomes a play within the play—played inside a mirror—and the dumb show for the *Murder of Gonzago* (played for the king and queen seated in the auditorium of the theatre itself) is a dumb show of Hamlet's story, not the Gonzago story. At any rate, as the first step in the dialectic, Hamlet's struggle places him squarely onstage, making his reality in defiance of the ones thrust on him.

In *Macbeth* conditions are substantially different. In the face of a world again deprived of sense or purpose, Macbeth takes a very different course. It is not so much an act of making spectacle or of intellectualizing but of sweeping, challenging brutality. In an amorphous world of uncertainty, darkness, and murk, the witches' prophesies compel Macbeth to create his own almost solipsistic reality, taking the tack of hastening the prophesies by any means available.

Henry IV brings the dialectic to a somewhat tentative conclusion. If in *Hamlet* the attempt had been to answer the world's empty unrewarding spectacle *with* spectacle and in *Macbeth* to usurp meaning through brutal action, here the response is double edged, played out between Falstaff and Hal, the one representing hedonistic abandon and the other pragmatic acceptance. In the process reason and poetry reclaim their place in the scheme of things. This is also a reclaiming of theatre itself. It first appears schizophrenic but ultimately proves to be homogeneous. The theatre (and the world as well) reasserts itself, and one can relax in the pleasure of theatre (cf. Allegri 1983, 14–16).

The Collettivo's dialectic also manifests itself in the manipulation of stage space. *Hamlet* is played on a bare stage (presented as just that), cluttered with all the trappings associated with a stage not in use—chairs, flats, and the brick back wall adorned only with the stenciled warning *"Vietato Fumare"* (No Smoking). Although the performers often acknowledge the audience, the stage itself is treated as an *encasement,* a kind of "Beckettian box" that metaphorically uses the stage to represent all of life, or at least all of rotten Denmark. It is a Chinese box, as well, for the stage contains other stages: one set up for the Gonzago play and others created by internal devices and action, such as a curious scene in Ophelia's grave played out by Horatio and Yorick for Hamlet as spectator or the madness of Ophelia played out in the frame of a mirror watched by Claudius and Laertes. The encasement, however, is total. The characters must remain in their places, lit by the harsh light of the sun in the form of a beam projector. They cannot leave.

The stage space for *Macbeth* is vastly different. The audience can faintly make out its full dimensions under its bluish bath of light. Like *Hamlet,* it is a self-contained space, but it differs in that we see the action as flashes of images; now here, now there. It is a cinematic world rather than a stage world. It is a world that behaves as though it were the *only* world, occupying a diegetic space that films occupy, incapable of responding to anything outside itself. This encourages Macbeth and Lady Macbeth to push their confines to the breaking point. When that happens, lights come up in the house and not only are we, the audience, reminded that we are in a theatre, but Macbeth must suffer the realization that there is more to the world than he had reckoned. Throughout the play characters create their own distinct places merely by turning on freestanding studio spotlights wherever they may be found in the theatre space.

The use of space in *Henry IV* is more subtle and intriguing than in either of the other two plays of the trilogy. The spectator enters an open rectangular space with seating on three sides and a tent in red brocade with gold embroidery on the fourth. Along the side of the open acting space are cafe tables and chairs at which the audience may choose to sit. There are no barriers between the acting and seating areas. Entering from the backside of the tent, the audience member can see the trappings for the show: costumes, props, a couple of motorcycles, a juke box, and so forth. Although there is a deliberate blurring of the distinction between the world of the play and that of the audience, there is nevertheless no confusion as to roles: the actors remain actors, the audience, audience.

The space itself is divided between that of the tent, illuminated with strong footlights, and the open space, which becomes the area for Falstaff and company. There is no fixed allocation of these spaces: the tent generally is the royal house and the open space the tavern, but there are times when action in the tavern spills over into the tent and others when royal activity moves forward into the open space. The actors are sometimes seen not only as characters but simply as actors awaiting their cue. Moreover, audience members sitting at the tables become, by extension, members of Falstaff's company. Battle is waged throughout the theatre space—around, behind, and among the spectators. This is essentially mansion and platea staging, with the tent as backdrop and as a staging area for the beginning and ending of scenes. This third play in the dialectic then—moving from the contained box of *Hamlet* to the cinematic play of images of *Macbeth* to the environmental space of *Henry IV*—opens up the space and more directly and fully engages the audience.

In another variation on the dialectic, the Collettivo created what I referred to earlier as metacharacters, those who move into and out of the fictional worlds of the play. They are reminders of the forces that are at work in a larger context. They are also conductors and facilitators of the action by their announcing scenes and transforming themselves into different characters within the plays. In *Hamlet* the metacharacter is Yorick. He is the thread that pulls together all the fragments of the spectacle. He is a court fool, a clown, an Arlecchino, who wanders through the play putting an ironic edge on it. He is his own grave digger, digging up his own bones. He stands both within and outside the story. He is linked to Horatio, who also functions as a sort of narrator, making the whole play a flashback. He is the metatheatrical "unleasher."

In *Macbeth* the metacharacter is the witch who launches the play from the auditorium, continues as narrator/chorus, and assumes multiple roles. She runs interference, disturbs the equilibrium of the world of the play, and introduces comic buffoonery. She is the traditional Vice character but rendered in unfamiliar terms as a punk wearing a gray jacket (with a great quantity of gloves hanging on it), black trousers, pink-and-green hair, a crooked beak for a nose, a gas mask, a Turkish pistol in a holster, three pairs of glasses, and a wooden sword. She loses most of these as the show progresses. She transforms into a messenger, the porter, and the German doctor who diagnoses Lady Macbeth's condition. She is always the Other, often coming onstage through the auditorium. She has a partner who operates inside the world of the play. He is first the prologue/chorus, then narrator and stagehand, then generic nobleman, then Malcolm, and finally the epilogue who speaks of the meaning of the play and turns out the lights.

Finally, in *Henry IV* the metacharacter—a female figure who moves through the entire spectacle—is somewhat more abstract. She wears black with red high heels and is a figure of death and an embodiment of the force of history. But she also becomes Lola, Falstaff's woman; the counter of the dead on the battlefield; a cashier at the tavern; and the attendant who covers the dead king's face with a cloth. She is a subtle disturbance to the action of the play. In the final moments she rises and stands in the tent behind Hal, now King Henry V, suggesting the inexorable power of history to pluck us up and dictate our roles.

Much of the vitality of these productions is achieved through the inventive use of anachronism. Throughout the plays one is constantly jolted out of complacency born of watching a remote masterpiece by abrupt insertions of items, customs, idioms, and attitudes that belong to our own time. In *Hamlet* these include the begging of Yorick and

Horatio in the auditorium for a hundred *lire,* the transformation of Hecuba to Cuba in Hamlet's reflection on the actors, and a pistol shot when Yorick finishes off King Claudius; in *Macbeth,* the witch's issuing her prophesy from the auditorium, then climbing onto the stage and asking an actor for a cigarette, and later (for the coronation of Macbeth and his Lady) the courtiers, dressed as modern bourgeois citizens, parading past the royal couple who watch their own ceremony on television. Finally, in *Henry IV* we see the hoodlums of the Eastcheap tavern riding around on motorcycles, playing soccer with empty drink cans, and playing billiards stretched out on the stage floor that serves as their billiard table.

Anachronism is part and parcel of the device of transformation that lets actors change from one character to another and objects stand in for imagined objects. The same actress is Ophelia and Gertrude; Claudius dons armor to become the ghost; Yorick and Horatio transform into Rosencrantz and Guildenstern; and Yorick digs up his own skull. The witch conducts us through the world of *Macbeth* but also transforms herself into the porter, and puppets act out the nightmares of Macbeth. Throughout the play we see actors transforming themselves and the scene in preparation for the next episode. In *Henry IV* a display of kendo (the martial art) represents a battle, the abstract female figure assumes multiple roles, and the characters find themselves constantly pushed into playing roles they hadn't bargained for.

The trilogy was developed between 1979 and 1981 and since then has toured widely. After the original performances in Parma, the Collettivo presented its spectacle in France, Germany, Holland, in major European cities such as Zurich, London, Dublin, and Brussels, and at the Holland Festival in June of 1982, where it attracted considerable critical international attention. Michael Coveney of the *Financial Times,* who saw the Collettivo there and subsequently traveled to Parma to see them, wrote of his experience: "From four o'clock last Saturday afternoon until just past one the next morning, I experienced one of the most exciting days I have spent in the theatre for a very long time." In the same article he continues:

> One of the great things about Shakespeare performed seriously and inventively in foreign languages is the liberation of Bardic mythology from our own traditions and expectations. Everyone has an *idea* of Hamlet, for instance, that is at least as potent as the fact of Hamlet. *Macbeth* is a play of superstition and atmosphere that quite supersedes the hard evidence of the English text. And *Henry IV* deals in issues of political choice that reverberate beyond the terms Shakespeare defines. The whole point of the-

atrical performance is, in a way, that of critical interpretation, not rever-
ential reproduction of a poetic package. (Coveney 1982)

When the Collettivo played at London's Riverside Studios in August
of 1983, Michael Billington of the *Guardian* reviewed the performance:

> Experimental Shakespeare is always more enjoyable in a language you don't
> understand: you don't mind what is done to the text. Purists will doubtless
> be dismayed. But anyone who wants to see an exuberant collective offering
> a gloss on Shakespeare will enjoy the experience. And the production is
> full of invention: a comic drill scene, a floor-length game of bar billiards
> being played as Hal and Falstaff do their Eastcheap role exchange, a ritual
> fight between Hal and Hotspur like something out of the Seven Samurai
> and a jazz piano tinkling in the background as Falstaff reflects on honour.
> (Billington 1983)

The trilogy, which the Collettivo has revived on numerous occasions,
is perhaps the company's most significant work. It has elicited international attention. This has happened not only by virtue of the spellbind-
ing nature of its spectacle but also because the work so richly embodies
the changing times of the 1970s and beyond. It is a theatrical signpost
on the road that takes us from the earlier experiments in the theatre
of cruelty, the theatre of the absurd, happenings and environmental
theatre, and epic theatre into postmodern explorations of fragmentation, multiplication of focus, interchangeable characters, anachronism,
and so-called contextual relativism. It is perhaps no accident that the
word *deconstruction* has come to mean so many more things in these
last two to three decades.

Works Cited

Abel, Lionel. 1963. *Metatheatre: A New View of Dramatic Form.* New York: Hill
and Wang.
Allegri, Luigi. 1983. "E se facessimo una commedia?" In *Tre Shakespeare della
Compagnia del Collettivo/Teatro Due,* ed. Luigi Allegri, pp. 11–95. Florence:
Liberoscambio.
Artaud, Antonin. 1958. *The Theatre and Its Double.* Trans. Mary Caroline
Richards. New York: Grove Press.
Billington, Michael. 1983. Review of *Henry IV. Guardian,* 19 August (clipping).
Brecht, Bertolt. 1964. "A Short Organum for the Theatre." In *Brecht on Theatre,*
ed. John Willett, pp. 179–205. New York: Hill and Wang.
Coveney, Michael. 1982. Review of the Progetto Shakespeare. *Financial Times,*
2 December (clipping).
Dall'Aglio, Gigi. 1983. "Nota della Compagnia del Collettivo." In *Tre Shake-*

speare della Compagnia del Collettivo/Teatro Due, ed. Luigi Allegri, pp. 99–
145. Florence: Liberoscambio.

———. 1989. Interview, Parma, Italy. 8 July.

Kott, Jan. 1966. *Shakespeare, Our Contemporary.* Trans. Boleslaw Taborski. Gar-
den City, N.Y.: Anchor Books.

"Shakespeare Project, 1979/1982." 1982. Brochure of the Compagnia del
Collettivo/Teatro Due.

Castillo

The Making of a
Postmodern Political Theatre

Dan Friedman

Margins, as in "Theatre at the Margins," the topic of this conference, and avant-garde, as in "The Avant Garde and Social Change: 1900–Present," the title of this panel, are two strikingly distinct metaphors for the social and cultural location of the theatre we are examining this weekend. The differences between these two images—margin and avant-garde—tell us much, I believe, about the differences between modernism and postmodernism in general and between the modernist political theatre of the twentieth century and the emerging work of the Castillo Theatre in New York City.

Avant-garde (the advanced guard) is a term tied to the concept of progress. To be in advance implies that there is a line of march, a movement forward, a pattern of continuing change and development that the advance guard is pioneering. Historically, avant-garde theatre has been theatre that has led, or conceived of itself as leading, the development of theatre. In addition, many avant-garde theatre artists in the twentieth century believed that their theatre could effect change in social attitudes, beliefs, and perceptions and actively strove to ally their work with the political avant-garde. At the end of the twentieth century, however, the political avant-garde has been discredited, and the theatre, even its most advanced and sophisticated components, does not appear to have had much impact on the bloody course of the century's history.

The margin, I would argue, is an image much more in sync with our times, with the social and political realities of the post-Communist, postpolitical world—a world that doesn't appear to be going forward or, for that matter, anywhere at all. It's also more in sync with postmodernism as an intellectual movement that has, after all, called into question the assumptions of progress, of linear causality, and, indeed, of the distinction between art and reality. Postmodernism presents a serious challenge to the artistic and social functions of the traditional avant-garde (an odd but accurate oxymoron) and to those theatre makers who have dedicated their lives to what used to be called political theatre.

The Castillo Theatre, of which I am a founder and the dramaturg, persists in being a political theatre in our seemingly apolitical age. Castillo is a sixteen-year-old, off-off-Broadway theatre in New York City. It is a political theatre without an ideology; that is, it is a political theatre that makes no pretense to having political answers. Castillo produces plays that attempt to challenge the underlying philosophical and political assumptions of our society, not because it has clearly formulated alternatives to these assumptions but as part of an ongoing social dialogue on human development. At the same time, it approaches performance itself as a developmental activity.

Although Castillo's philosophical/political concerns and its approach to performance may distinguish it from most other off-off-Broadway theatres, Castillo artists don't see their work as being the advance guard of anything. In fact, they don't believe that theatre, in and of itself, can effect social change at all. The avant-garde and progressive political theatre have historically shared the assumption that the emotional and/or cogitative impact of a production on an audience could somehow lead to a change in consciousness that would then lead the audience (or some members of the audience) to alter their behavior outside the theatre. This approach to theatre as a tool-for-result or, in the lingo of the 1960s, as a "consciousness raising" activity appears to Castillo to have proven ineffective. Castillo approaches theatre not as consciousness raising or pedagogy but as part and parcel of a larger organizing and community-building effort. Instead of trying to change people's minds, or get them to think, or move them to action, Castillo works to create a shared performatory experience. Theatre, the Castillo company is convinced, can do no more than that, but that, they feel strongly, is worth doing. This experience, then, is not a tool *for* any result; it is, rather a tool *and* result simultaneously.[1] The experience is what it is; people do various things with experiences.

---

[1]The distinction between "tool-for-result" and "tool-and-result" was first articulated in Fred Newman and Lois Holzman, *Lev Vygotsky: Revolutionary Scientist* (New York: Routledge, 1993).

In a culture such as ours, in which theatre is regarded either as a commodity that must yield a profit or as high art that should be subsidized by corporate or government funds, Castillo, a sort of rough-and-tumble community theatre for all New York City, finds itself on the margin. It is not that Castillo is on the margin of society. In many ways Castillo is far more integrated into the mainstream of daily life than most theatres. Rather, Castillo is a theatre on the margins of the *institution* of theatre—a location, it believes, that is precisely where a political theatre can be most useful in the contemporary world. Why is this so? Castillo believes that being on the margin means being in touch with the mainstream, as well as everything that is not mainstream. It means being able to cross the border between what is and what might be.

Castillo's marginality is therefore a key to both its politics and its art. By deconstructing Castillo's marginality we can, perhaps, begin to grapple with how it is possible to be a political theatre at a point in history when most people are deeply cynical about politics and when hardly anyone goes to the theatre.

Central to Castillo's marginality is the marginality of its creators. Most of the people who founded and built Castillo were not trained theatre people. Instead, they were, and have remained, community organizers and progressive political activists even as they developed rather sophisticated theatre skills. Fred Newman, Castillo's artistic director and playwright-in-residence, for example, emerged from the radical therapy movement of the 1960s. A philosopher by training, Newman was initially drawn to the countercultural and political movements of the 1960s because of their promise of transforming both the personal and the political and their insistence that the two were part of the same totality.

While other radical therapy movements in the 1970s were building alternative psychologies, Newman and his colleagues were building an alternative *to* psychology. The difference between what Newman built, which has come to be called *performance social therapy,* and psychology, in all its variations, is the former's insistence that human emotionality and development are social activities, not inner psychic phenomena. The unit of study in performance social therapy is the group, not the individual, and the curative (developmental) process is social, activistic, and performatory, not intrapsychic and analytic.[2]

---

[2]For an introduction to the theoretical and practical relevance of social therapy see Holzman (1999) and Newman (1994).

Newman's work in therapy was never an end in itself. Instead, it was approached as one component in a general effort to create environments in which development might be reignited and encouraged. During the last twenty-five years Newman and an expanding circle of colleagues and collaborators have been involved in a wide range of organizing efforts, in unions, in welfare centers, in schools, and in independent electoral politics. Newman's engagement of the institutions of psychology and of culture are related to the extent that they both have grown out of the somewhat obvious, but all-too-often ignored, realization that it is not possible to qualitatively change the world if the would-be changers (human beings) can't find a way to change themselves in the process.

In the course of a quarter century of organizing, Newman has exposed the old notion of a political avant-garde as both ineffective and elitist. What he, Castillo, and other ongoing projects have created instead of a "vanguard" is an international, multicultural, political and cultural community—an experimental community, both deeply integrated into the mainstream of society and, because of its interest in the transformation of society, on the margins.

The Castillo Theatre has been one of the outcomes of this community building. As a group of community builders whose theatre activity emerged from that organizing process, Castillo, unlike earlier political and avant-garde theatres, cannot be characterized as a theatre trying to bring art to the people. It might better be described as social organizing carried on by theatrical means. Castillo's very existence as a thriving political theatre outside the nonprofit funding network (and largely indifferent to the aesthetic concerns of the avant-garde) is, on one level, a provocation. It refuses to "play the game" and thus challenges the institutional assumptions of the theatre itself, much as performance social therapy challenges the institution of psychology.

Coming to theatre from community organizing and radical therapy has had many consequences—artistically, structurally, and politically—on the evolution of Castillo's theatre work. Since the mid-1980s Castillo has produced eighty-four plays and musicals by eighteen playwrights. The playwrights have been women and men, gay and straight, African American, Chicano, Puerto Rican, and white; from the United States, Germany, Austria, Switzerland, Israel, India, and Martinique. Among those who have directed at Castillo are Yusef Mundi, the late gadfly of the Israeli theatre, and Stephan Suschke, a protégé of Heiner Müller and, until late last year, an artistic director at the Berliner Ensemble. Castillo's operating budget in the last fiscal year was $419,403, with slightly over half its income generated from ticket sales and the rest from grassroots fund-raising. It has a subscription base of a little less

Dostoyevsky's *Notes from Underground*), dying of a mysterious disease, argues with his sister, Spintze, a member of the Jewish Socialist Bund, about politics, death, and identity—and late-twentieth-century America, where Sam, an African American dying of AIDS, argues with his sister, Pearlie, a black nationalist, about similar issues. As the play progresses, characters from the nineteenth century start appearing (in slightly altered forms) in the twentieth-century scenes, and it becomes unclear who is dead and who is alive (and what those labels mean). By the end, as Riven and Sam encounter each other in a bar, it's not even clear that they are separate people. The individual as a distinctly defined unit of human existence is not, in *What Is to Be Dead?* (and in other Newman plays), taken for granted as it is in the bulk of Western dramatic (and other) literature.

Although *What Is to Be Dead?* raises many questions, people looking for answers will not find them in the production. The action of the play is, among other things, a prolonged asking of the question "What Is to Be Dead?" It, like most work done by Castillo, attempts no answer.

These three plays are not in any way an exhaustive account of the twenty-six scripts by Newman that have been produced at Castillo. Still less should they be considered representative of the eighty-four plays written by eighteen different playwrights that have been staged by the Castillo Theatre over sixteen years. They are referenced in some detail here because they *do* represent, in terms of content, what might be regarded as the three major *types* of plays—the topical, the historical, and the philosophical—for which Castillo is most noted. Each *type* is political in the broadest sense of the word; that is, each grapples with power relations among humans and/or examines the assumptions by which we live. (It is important to note that these labels are applied in retrospect. There has been no conscious categorization on the part of Castillo's artists). Stylistically, Castillo borrows from (and mixes and matches) a number of avant-garde traditions and constantly raids popular culture.

Whatever one might think of this wide range of politically engaged productions, it is reasonable to assume that it would at least stir some interest among the official gatekeepers of the avant-garde. Yet Castillo's work has for the most part been stubbornly ignored. This marginalization, I would argue, has little to do with the form and content of Castillo's work, which, although decidedly idiosyncratic in the best sense of the word, is hardly "out of the ballpark" of contemporary theatre and drama. It has more to do with the noncommercial theatre establishment's attitudes toward the political histories of Castillo's founders and toward Castillo's refusal to seek funding through the usual channels open to nonprofit, resident theatre companies. This influence of New York City politics on the shape of New York's nonprofit theatre scene during the last two decades is worthy of a study itself. However, what is important here is the fact of Castillo's marginalization by New York's theatre establishment.

Despite this enforced marginalization, Castillo's audience and financial base have continued to expand. Castillo is, by all quantifiable standards, thriving. It is thriving on the margins because it has developed a fund-raising and audience-building model adapted to the margin. Early in its history Castillo made a simple, and in some ways insane, decision. It decided to go to the people, most of whom, after all, also exist on the margin of the institution of the theatre. The Castillo collective decided to canvass door-to-door every day in diverse communities in the New York metropolitan area and ask people to contribute to the building of a theatre that would be free of government and corporate strings. If the communities of New York were willing to support its work, Castillo would exist; if they weren't, there would be no Castillo theatre.

Since 1989 over 450,000 people have given $10 or more to Castillo and its performatory sister projects, and today virtually all of its shows sell out in advance. This is because a core of dedicated volunteers—some theatre people, some not, but all community organizers—have taken collective responsibility for the development of the theatre, a responsibility that includes constant outreach and fund-raising. In recent years Castillo has transitioned from canvassing and street work to a telemarketing operation.

This is Castillo's most obviously marginal activity. Theatre artists simply don't stand on subway platforms raising money. It is unheard of and unseemly. Most theatre people, when they hear of this tactic, shake their heads in disbelief. Yet it is precisely this marginal activity that puts Castillo squarely in the middle of New York life. Its primary audience isn't the small pool of people who would go to the theatre anyway. Castillo's audience comes to the theatre because it has been *organized* to come by meeting someone involved with Castillo in person or on the phone or in some other community context. In this way Castillo has literally created its audience person by person. It is a diverse audience and one that, for the most part, is new to the theatre. On any given night you might find in Castillo's seventy-one-seat theater a married couple from New Jersey sitting next to guys from a homeless shelter sitting next to a gay couple from Chelsea sitting next to a group of hip-hoppers from the Bronx sitting next to black church ladies from Brooklyn.

Is this a marginal audience? In terms of the theatre world, where the audience is overwhelmingly white, over forty-five years old, and upper middle class, it certainly is. Yet it is far more representative of the general population of New York City and of the people with whom a political theatre would arguably want to be involved. From the periphery, Castillo has built an audience representing a broad cross section of New York City's population, and in the process boundaries began to be redefined.

Castillo's economic and political independence and supportive audience have allowed it to take many artistic and political risks that would be very difficult to take anywhere but on the margin. First, it should be noted that although Castillo's productions raise political and philosophical questions, our playwrights and directors work hard *not* to answer them, as demonstrated in the case of *What Is to Be Dead?*, for example. In terms of content this is primarily what distinguishes Castillo from earlier politically engaged theatres and theatre movements (naturalism, Socialist realism, agitprop, epic theatre) that, perceiving themselves to be a part of the advance guard, worked to provide, or at least point in the direction of, answers.

Not only does Castillo not provide answers; it also works *not* to provide plots. In fact, as touched on in the discussion of both *Crown Heights* and *Sally and Tom*, Castillo considers the subversion of narrative to be one of its artistic and political tasks. Why? Because, as a number of postmodernists have noted, in Western culture since the Greeks, humans have looked at and understood themselves, individually and collectively, through stories. Stories have predetermined shapes, outcomes, resolutions, and implicit meanings that are historically constructed within a particular social/cultural continuum, and they almost always support the world-as-it-is. Even plots in which the protagonists rebel against the world-as-it-is support conserving the narrative framework.

Castillo artists maintain that plots/stories/narratives, no matter *what* their content, limit the possibilities for development. The conservatizing propagandistic element of the theatre as an institution—in the formal, not just substantive, sense—is that it reinforces this sense of our lives as stories. Narrative, Castillo believes, is what keeps us from performing creatively in day-to-day life. It restrains us as characters, so to speak, in somebody else's story. Instead of offering the audience new narratives (that is, new role possibilities), Castillo seeks to offer the possibility of life without narrative—a possibility that demands constructing our lives in a more active, creative (i.e., performatory) way. That, more than the content of any particular play, is where the "politicalness"—and the postmodernism—of Castillo is to be found.

Castillo's political postmodernism is also evident in its approach to character and performance. In many of its plays, particularly those by Newman, character is rarely a stable, clearly defined entity. The perimeters between you and him and her and me are fluid, porous, constantly shifting. The audience comes wanting to identify with the characters, but identification is difficult because the characters are not ontologically stable; they disappear and reemerge and transform. There are no permanent roles. As in performance social therapy, the focus is on the development of the group, the ensemble, not the individual as a self-contained entity.

This not only puts a demand on the audience to see character in a new way. It also places a demand on actors to find new ways of performing. The actor at Castillo is not encouraged to get "inside" or to "the bottom" of a character. As far as Castillo's directors are concerned, there is no inside or bottom to get to. Instead, the work is to discover the interconnectedness between the characters. The acting activity is not, therefore, an inner journey into a closed entity (either the character's or the actor's psyche); it is instead a social (interactive) journey into transformation.

One of the most important interconnections explored on Castillo's stage is the relationship between the actor and the character. In all theatre there is a dialectic between the actor as actor and the actor as character, with, for example, Stanislavsky and Brecht placing emphasis on different aspects of this dialectic. The traditional goal of the rehearsal process is, among other things, to cover over that dialogue by opening night so that the actor has, as far as the audience can tell, "become the character." In Castillo's productions the director and the actors, much closer to Brecht than Stanislavsky in this regard, work to keep the dialogue open and obvious to the audience throughout the run of the play.

However, this concentration on developing and exposing the relationship between the actor and the character is not for Castillo, as it is for Brecht, a means of helping the audience reflect on ideas within the confines of the theatre. Instead, it is approached as a means of subverting the very boundaries of theatre itself, by blurring (and eventually obliterating) the distinction between theatre and everyday life. It is Castillo's hope that the audience member, by becoming aware of the creative tension between actor and character, can come to identify performance not with a set of acting conventions and skills but with the activity of showing people who you are and who you are not at the same time, an activity that anyone, regardless of talent, can do anywhere.

Castillo's ongoing organizing activity, if you will, is to liberate performance from the theatre. Those involved in the Castillo experiment are convinced—and this has its roots in their collective experience as community organizers and as performance social therapists, as well as theatre artists—that performance, the ability to simultaneously be both who you are and who you are not, can be a developmental activity, off-stage as well as on.

Which brings us again to Castillo's particular relationship with its audience, with its community. After all, neither Castillo's political concerns nor its aesthetic particulars (plotless plays, emergent characters, and a nonpsychological approach to acting) are unique to Castillo. What is unique is the relationship of all these performatory activities to a growing community.

Castillo is not a new type of theatre. It is simply a theatre that recognizes the performatory dimension of human life. It is not of the avant-garde; it has made no discovery about the theatre per se. Its discovery, if there is one, is about the relationship between theatre and everyday life. Castillo functions on the margins of the theatre, where performance overlaps with community building, therapy, and politics. It transgresses the borders of all these social spheres, and in so doing, its organizers maintain, it opens up new possibilities for creative human development.

Castillo does not view its accomplishments as being in any way a refutation of the avant-garde. The artists of the avant garde, Castillo believes, have labored long and hard to "push the envelope," to produce theatre in new and provocative ways. In so doing they have provided Castillo and all theatre artists with invaluable tools. That their work has failed to stimulate the kind of social change many of them hoped for is hardly their fault. It is, rather, a limitation of the theatre itself.

Castillo doesn't seek to use theatre to provoke social change. Rather it uses the theatre as a launching pad to organize performatory social activity. Will this performatory social activity play a role in changing the world? As postmodernists, all the artists of Castillo will say is that they have no way of knowing. Knowing itself, they maintain, is suspect in the theatre, an art and an activity that at its best has the potential to explore human possibility, not merely mimic a fixed reality.

Works Cited

Holzman, Lois, ed. 1999. *Performing Psychology: A Postmodern Culture of the Mind*. New York: Routledge.

Newman, Fred. 1994. *Let's Develop! A Guide to Continuous Personal Growth*. New York: Castillo International.

Contributors

Oscar G. Brockett is Professor of Theatre and Dance and holder of the Z. T. Scott Family Chair in Drama at the University of Texas at Austin. He is the author of ten books—including *History of the Theatre, The Essential Theatre,* and *Century of Innovation*—and more than fifty articles. He is past recipient of a Guggenheim Fellowship, a Fulbright Fellowship, and numerous career achievement awards. Dr. Brockett is a member of the Academy of Distinguished Teachers and was awarded the Robert Lewis Medal for Lifetime Achievement in Theatre Research and the E. W. Doty Award.

David Callaghan is Assistant Professor of Theatre at the University of Montevallo. He has written extensively about the Living Theatre and 1960s avant-garde theatre in publications such as *Theatre Journal* and the *Journal of Dramatic Theory and Criticism.* His interests include plays and films about the Vietnam War and theatrical and cinematic representations of race, culture, and gender.

Jonathan Chambers is Assistant Professor of Speech and Theatre at St. Lawrence University, where he teaches performance studies and acting. He has presented his work at ATHE and MATC and has published in *Victorian Studies* and *Theatre History Studies.* His areas of interest include early-twentieth-century American drama and theatre of the political left, Michael Chekhov, the historical avant-garde, and melodrama as a period acting style.

Mark J. Charney is Associate Professor at Clemson University, where he heads the film program in the English Department and serves as Graduate Director for both the master of arts in English and the master's program in Professional Communication. Dr. Charney has been active in the American College Theatre Festival, currently serves as Chair of the Critics' Institute, and will begin a three-year term as Chair of Region IV in 2001. He has published a biographical/critical look at the writing of southern novelist Barry Hannah and is presently working on an analytical study of *Schindler's List* for Cambridge University Press.

Dan Friedman is the dramaturg of the Castillo Theatre in New York City, which he helped to found sixteen years ago. He is editor of *Still on the Corner and Other Postmodern Political Plays by Fred Newman* and coeditor, with Bruce McConachie, of *Theatre for Working-Class Audiences in the United States, 1830–1980.* Dr. Friedman is also the author of fourteen plays. He earns his living as a journalist.

James M. Harding is Assistant Professor of English at Mary Washington College. He is the author of *Adorno and "A Writing of the Ruins": Essays on Modern Aesthetics and Anglo-American Literature and Culture* and the forthcoming *Contours of the Theatrical Avant-Garde: Performance and Textuality.* Dr. Harding has also published in numerous journals and is working on two books: *The Liberal Theatre and the Radical Spectator: Explorations in the Limits of Contemporary Political Theatre* and *The Modern Poet as Playwright: Critical Theory and the Politics of Lyrical Performance.*

John H. Houchin directs and teaches theatre history, American theatre, experimental theatre, and acting at Boston College. His research has been published in *The Drama Review,* the *Journal of American Drama and Theatre,* the *New England Theatre Journal,* and *Theatre History Studies.* He is currently writing a book, *Under Siege: The History of American Theatrical Censorship in the Twentieth Century.*

Martha S. LoMonaco is Associate Professor of Visual and Performing Arts and Director of the Theatre Program at Fairfield University in Connecticut. She is an active director, having premiered new works in New York City, New England, and at the Edinburgh Fringe Festival. Dr. LoMonaco is the author of numerous articles, as well as the book *Every Week, a Broadway Revue: The Tamiment Playhouse, 1921–1960.*

Stanley Vincent Longman is Professor of Drama at the University of Georgia, where he is in charge of the playwriting program. In addition, he conducts a summer-studies-abroad program based in Parma, Italy, and London, England. He was editor of *Theatre Symposium* for the 1997 and 1998 volumes and is the author of a text on playwriting, *Composing Drama for Stage and Screen.*

Robert I. Lublin is a Ph.D. candidate in the University of Texas at Austin's Theatre in History, Criticism, and Theory program. Mr. Lublin is the book review and performance review editor for *Theatre InSight,* a former research assistant and assistant editor of *The Cambridge History of American Theatre,* a past editor of *Concept: Graduate Journal of Interdisciplinary Research,* and a recipient of the *AGON* Creative Writing Award for Poetry.

Mark E. Mallett is Assistant Professor of Theater at Morehead State University and serves as a co-director of the Kentucky Institute for Arts in Education, a multidisciplinary, two-week, graduate credit/professional development arts and humanities workshop for in-service public school teachers. Before entering teaching, Dr. Mallett worked as a lighting designer, stage manager, and production manager for various ballet companies.

Mark S. Weinberg is Professor of Communication and Theatre Arts and Director of Theatre at the University of Wisconsin, Rock County. He was a member of the *Other Theatre Company* collective in the 1980s and has studied and written about collectively organized and socially conscious theatre for over twenty years, most extensively in his book *Challenging the Hierarchy: Collective Theatre in the United States.* More recently he has been exploring political issues in performance, popular culture, and pedagogy. He has studied with Augusto Boal and has conducted workshops (some with colleague Doug Paterson) for educators, students, and activists in the United States, Canada, and Australia using Theatre of the Oppressed techniques.